ORANGECOUNTYCHOPPERS™

THE TALE OF THE TEUTULS

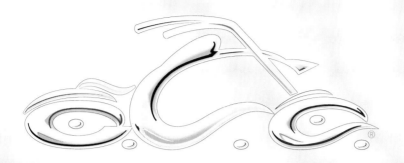

ORANGE**COUNTY**CHOPPERS™

THE TALE OF THE TEUTULS

BY
PAUL TEUTUL SR.
PAUL M. TEUTUL AND
MICHAEL TEUTUL

WITH
KEITH AND KENT ZIMMERMAN

WARNER BOOKS

NEW YORK   BOSTON

Warner Books
Hachette Book Group USA
1271 Avenue of the Americas
New York, NY 10020

Visit our Web site at www.HachetteBookGroupUSA.com.

Printed in Canada

First Edition: October 2006

10   9   8   7   6   5   4   3   2   1

Warner Books and the "W" logo are trademarks of Time Warner Inc. or an affiliated company. Used under license by Hachette Book Group USA, which is not affiliated with Time Warner Inc.

Orange County Choppers, the initials O.C.C., and the O.C.C. motorcycle
design logo and related inditia are trademarks of Orange County Choppers
Design Properties, LLC.

Library of Congress Cataloging-in-Publication Data

Teutul, Paul Sr.
   Orange county choppers : the tale of the Teutuls / Paul Teutul Sr., Paul M. Teutul, and Michael
Teutul with Keith and Kent Zimmerman. — 1st ed.
      p. cm.
   ISBN-13: 978-0-446-52801-6
   ISBN-10: 0-446-52801-3
   1. Teutul, Paul, Sr. 2. Teutul, Paul, Jr. 3. Teutul, Mike. 4. Motorcyclists—United States—
Biography. 5. American chopper (Television program) 6. Motorcycles—Customizing. 7. Orange
County (New York)—Biography. I. Teutul, Paul, Jr. II. Teutul, Mike. III. Zimmerman, Keith.
IV. Zimmerman, Kent, 1953– V. Title.
   TL440.2.T48 2006
   629.227'50922—dc22

                                                                                    2006016347

DEDICATION

To life's opportunities

ACKNOWLEDGMENTS

Writing this book gave us the rare opportunity to look back on what we've been able to accomplish over the years since our "overnight" success. It was a great experience reminiscing with family, friends, and staff in preparation for this book. It was also a valuable way to help us plot our future. We learned a lot about ourselves writing this book. We hope our fans, friends, and customers are equally inspired reading it.

Never underestimate the importance of family. We'd like to acknowledge and thank our family members, particularly Helen, Paula, Cristin, and Dan. It was great sitting down and telling stories. Thank you for your input in filling in the missing pieces with your pictures and remembrances. We'd also like to acknowledge Craig Piligian and his staff at Pilgrim Films. Thanks to the Discovery Channel executives, and to Billy Campbell and Jane Root. We'd also like to thank the OCC staff for everything they do on a daily basis in moving the company toward greater things.

Also, a big thank-you to the ZimmerMEN, Scott Waxman and Farley Chase. Thanks to Colin Fox for his direction and guidance.

The Zimmermen wish to acknowledge the Teutul family, who made us feel welcome and gave us unbelievable access to their operations as well as unflinchingly honest discourse. We had a blast working with you guys. We especially thank Senior, Junior, Mike, Paula, Danny, Cristin, and Helen. Steve Moreau, Michele Paolella, Scott Waxman, Jason Pohl, Craig Piligian, Colin Fox, Farley Chase, Scott Amann, Ron Salsbury, Rick Petko, Vinnie DiMartino, Jim Quinn, Martin GM Kelly, Joe Puliafico, John Sohigian, Jennifer Weyant, Celia Johnson, Pat Favata, and our family members, including Gladys & Deb, Nitin & Naveen Abraham, Doris & Joe Zimmerman, Sonny & Fritz, and everybody at H-Unit, San Quentin.

TABLE OF CONTENTS

ORANGECOUNTYCHOPPERS™

THE TALE OF THE
TEUTULS

The Teutul clan in front of Edinburgh Castle in Edinburgh, Scotland, filming episodes of **American Chopper** *in Great Britain, France, and Ireland. Left to right: Paulie, Mikey, and Senior. (Photo: Martin GM Kelly)*

CHAPTER 1

Senior and Paulie lie knocked out after a hard day signing at the breakthrough Louisiana Bike Expo in May 2003. (Photo: OCC Archives)

FROM THE BASEMENT
TO THE SUPERDOME

SENIOR:

I remember the day it went completely nuts. The first real blowout. Louisiana Bike Expo. May 3, 2003. New Orleans Superdome. Everything clicked into place. That Saturday afternoon, Orange County Choppers, a small upstate New York custom bike building shop that my son Paulie and I started in 1999 in the basement of my house, had just erupted. Like the ZZ Top song said, "We were bad, we were nationwide." We'd caught the attention of the American public.

When they'd introduced the Teutuls at the Bike Expo during a special presentation honoring firefighters and military veterans, we'd gotten mobbed as we slowly rode through the crowd. The throngs parted like the Red Sea. There were waves of smiling faces giving us the thumbs-up sign. Pocket cameras flashed in our faces. Paul Junior rode on the now famous Fire Bike. The Fire Bike was our fire-engine-red, rolling tribute to the brave men of FDNY who'd perished during the World Trade Center bombings on 9/11. I rode alongside Paulie on the Black Widow, a shining spooky *Creepshow*-style purple-and-black machine dripping with chrome spiderwebs that garnished the gas tank and the front and back fenders. As we threaded our way through the crowd, Paulie gunned the engine of the Fire Bike and sounded the alarm. Above the thunder and blustering torque of our chromed V-Twin motors blared an authentic fire truck siren we had mounted onto the Fire Bike. The rumble of both bikes echoed and bounced throughout the giant indoor stadium.

The crowd cheered us like a couple of comic-book superheroes. The heroic lineup of firefighters stood onstage alongside the military veterans who had served in the Vietnam War. It was an emotionally charged moment. The impact of motorcycles and firefighters and war heroes raised the pitch level even higher, inspiring the audience and us in a way I'll never, ever forget. At that moment, I realized our bikes could touch the hearts and minds of Americans in a way we'd never imagined in our wildest dreams.

Paulie (left) rides the Fire Bike as Senior revs up the Black Widow at the Louisiana Bike Expo. (Photo: OCC Archives)

When Discovery Networks first contacted us in 2002 about filming a television documentary, we thought it might be a much-needed shot in the arm to our tiny East Coast custom chopper operation. We had already seen the effect that television had on Jesse James and West Coast Choppers after Discovery aired his *Motorcycle Mania* show in 2001. We watched from afar at the various bike shows as people fussed over Jesse. He drew long lines of admirers buying T-shirts and hats while we were stuck in the back of the hall with our half a dozen basement-built bikes, that we trailered around the country. Jesse's newfound popularity gave us hope that someday we could achieve a fraction of that notoriety.

Then it happened to us.

On September 29, 2002, when the Discovery Channel aired the very first pilot episode of *American Chopper,* we scored over two million viewers out of the box. After four years of wrenching away in relative anonymity inside our Hudson Valley bike shop, after pushing and clawing for any bit of print exposure we could muster, we found our personal lives splashed across television. Not sure whether it was a statistical fluke or a one-shot deal, the Discovery people aired a second pilot on January 19, 2003—to equally high ratings. It seemed for real. America had instantly embraced a volatile father-and-son bike building team who mixed it up, argued and fought, and confronted each other aggressively on a dead Monday-night time slot—and on cable TV, no less.

The Fire Bike, honoring America's firefighters, is one of the most famous OCC theme bikes ever. Here it is drawing a crowd at the Superdome after the episode about it had just aired. (Photo: OCC Archives)

Fame was right around the corner, but we didn't know it. Another early sign came on February 28, 2003, two months prior to our Superdome appearance. We had rolled into Daytona Beach for Daytona Bike Week, expecting to sell a few bikes and hopefully score a couple of custom orders to keep our fledgling bike business going. Five hundred thousand motorcycle fans roared into Florida for Bike Week, and a lot of those people had apparently seen our TV pilot. We noticed things heating up. While the crowd reaction at Bike Week wasn't crazy-crazy, we got more attention than usual at a small meet-and-greet staged at Pompano Pat's bike shop in Daytona. Although it wasn't exactly pandemonium, there was a constant flow of people seeking autographs and handshakes. A year earlier, we'd walked through downtown and putted down Main Street anonymously. This time, people were shouting at us from their bikes and cars.

"Paul-ie!"

"Senior!"

We were stopped on the streets for photos and autographs. Recognition.

After the pilots had aired and a month after Daytona, on March 31, 2003, *American Chopper* debuted its first full season, after which we made another bike show appearance at the Javits Center in New York City. Again, things had kicked up a notch. Only this time we drew larger crowds as we displayed our current lineup of bikes. On top of that, after packing up, we found we actually netted some pretty decent scoot selling our own OCC merchandise.

But it was the 2003 Louisiana Bike Expo appearance that capped it. Five brand-new episodes of *American Chopper* had been rolled out and broadcast. Nobody predicted the excitement we would generate in New Orleans. Yet the night before was just another OCC road show gig for us. We trailered in our choppers and wheeled them ourselves into the Superdome loading dock on a Thursday night, after which we hosted a gathering with some fans at a bar and restaurant called The Dock. By Friday morning, we had a lineup of show bikes, including the Fire Bike, the Black Widow, the Cody Project, and Senior's Twelve Up chopper, set up prominently in the main exposition hall. Turns out our timing was perfect. We couldn't have planned things better.

By the time we hit New Orleans, the Fire Bike episode had just aired. The Louisiana Bike Expo attendees would be the first television fans to experience the Fire Bike up close and personal. Everybody from OCC, including Paulie, Mikey, Vinnie, Vinnie's dad, and I, was pretty pumped up. Although this was the first bike event that actively promoted us on the basis of our new cable TV show, everyone, including the organizers, was in shock at the eventual turnout. Endless lines of everyday people waited to meet us. After signing autographs for ten straight hours the first day, it seemed as if we'd barely put a dent in the demand. T-shirts, hats, and posters sold like hotcakes. So we signed for three days, nonstop. And still they came.

In the past, after a bike show, we could expect to return home with a bundle of unsold merch. This time, we'd arrived in New Orleans way underprepared. Five thousand T-shirts flew off the shelves in one day. We were in deep trouble. Running out of merchandise the first day was a mortal sin, so we enlisted a shop in New Orleans to rush-order more shirts. Ten times more T-shirts, because after Louisiana, we were moving on to another big bike show in Myrtle Beach, South Carolina. Like the Louisiana Bike Expo, the promoters capitalized on our new television show and gave our appearance headline status. We could expect bigger crowds there.

After signing for three consecutive ten-hour days in New Orleans, we signed for five more eight-hour days in Myrtle Beach. Seventy hours total, two venues, and several sore wrists and fingers and hands later, the crowds were still not satisfied. As tired as we were, we couldn't stop. Who knew? Our newfound celebrity as the father-and-son-cable-TV-bike-builders could end at any moment, possibly as quickly as it started.

What blew us away were the attendees. Families! Entire families were anxious to meet us in both New Orleans and Myrtle Beach. That puzzled us. It was the first time we'd noticed such an influx of families at bike shows. Families didn't show up at biker events. Not in full force, anyway. We'd struck a chord with both parents and their kids. Everybody could relate to us, not as bike builders, but as real people, as fathers and sons, whether the fans were men or women, even mothers and daughters.

And we were overwhelmed by the intensity of the crowd. Cancer victims. Terminally ill children. People in wheelchairs. Folks who couldn't stand or walk. They were there to see *us*, and willing to wait in a long line. It was astonishing, and we didn't want to let anybody down. Unaccustomed to the deluge, we were dizzy and physically woozy at the close of each appearance.

The end of our mini road trip physically and emotionally drained us. We were wiped out. We had nothing left to give. We felt like a couple of empty bottles. Smiling continuously for hours on end, our faces hurt. After hours of questions and handshakes, our hands were sore. Our voices were hoarse. Cameras and strobe lights flickered in front of our eyes all day long. It was disorienting, and it yanked away a piece of our psyche in a strange way. So this was fame?

Thanks to an off-the-wall cable television show and a loyal legion of newfound fans and fan families, it was looking as if we had vaulted for good out of the basement and into the hearts and minds of the American public. It was our first real introduction to prominence. And I'll be honest with you: It felt pretty damn good, because up to now, it had been a long strange trip for the Teutul family. Now, we wondered, what would be the ultimate cost of this fame?

CHAPTER 2

A rare childhood photo of Senior. That's him on the far right, at the beach. (Photo: OCC Archives)

TWO CENTS A WINDOW AND FIVE CENTS A DOOR

SENIOR:

Who would have thought it possible? A family of bike builders makes television history. Every Monday night at ten o'clock, millions of viewers tune in to find out what America's favorite dysfunctional family is up to. After the first three seasons, our TV show, *American Chopper,* turned into equal parts *I Love Lucy, Ozzie & Harriet, The Three Stooges, The Simpsons,* and *Monster Garage.* But instead of wrapping candy on a fast conveyor belt like Lucy, looking for tutti-frutti ice cream like Ozzie, slapping the crap out of each other like the Stooges, making Homer's life a misery like the Simpsons, or creating a hot rod out of a tractor like Jesse, we build custom bikes. Beautiful motorcycles. Choppers. Most important, though, every freakin' week we chase the American Dream. In front of millions of viewers.

Our family name is spelled T-E-U-T-U-L, pronounced *Tuttle.* We are the Teutuls, and I'm the father who yells all the time and loses his head.

My full name is Paul Teutul. When I was born and it came time to hand out middle names, I got passed over. Or so I thought. The guys around the OCC shop call me "Senior," and a lot of other things when I'm out of earshot. My oldest son, Paulie, christened Paul Michael Teutul, is known as "Junior." But in actual fact, Paulie and I aren't officially junior and senior at all. My youngest son, Mikey,

Michael Joseph Teutul, has always been . . . well . . . Mikey, although his sister Cristin calls him Michael. I have one other son named Danny.

We are the Teutuls.

To confuse matters further, my father was also named Paul. Paul John Teutul. Recently, after applying for a passport, I found out that I actually *did* have a middle name. It's John, just like my father, which, funny enough, makes *me* an official junior. But my parents didn't tell me I had a middle name, so they could distinguish between my father and me.

Go figure.

Our family bloodline is a mixture of German, Austrian, and Italian. My mom, Josephine DeVito, was pure Italian. We ate spaghetti every Sunday and steak every Saturday. That became our family tradition. That and a whole lot of shouting, arguing, and drinking.

My mother was the drinker in my family. Her parents were named Christina and John DeVito. She had four brothers and a sister. My uncles drank heavily, too. My grandfather was a wino-type drunk. He favored his sons and didn't like his daughter, so my mother was mistreated growing up. She didn't get along with her father.

My grandfather on my dad's side, John Teutul, came from German and Austrian stock. My grandmother, Lena, also came from Germany. She spoke nine languages, and I remember her speaking every one of them around the house. My grandparents were born in the Old Country back in Germany and were processed through Ellis Island as children. Both of them lived in New York City before they settled in Yonkers. Before I was born, while living in New York City, my grandfather owned and operated a pool hall and a restaurant. He was a tough son of a bitch who stood over six feet tall, lean and muscular. My old man told me stories of how my grandfather would throw guys down the front stairs of the poolroom if they gave him grief. You didn't want to piss him off; he could knock guys out with just one punch. Grandpa John Teutul gave the family clan its strict code, its work ethic, which exists to this day.

Work. Work. Work.

Then you work some more.

That's how it was when I grew up. I was born in Yonkers, New York, on May 1, 1949. I had four sisters: Christine, Beverly, Deborah, and Elaine. I was the only boy, the second oldest of the kids.

We lived in a brick house on 11 Cooper Street, a single-family house with an apartment downstairs. My grandfather had built it, and he lived a couple of doors down. He owned our house and two other houses on our block as well as two more six-apartment units on the corner. They were made of brick because he built things to last. And he built them himself before I was born. He mixed the concrete himself. Laid the bricks by hand. He used cheap labor, including my father when he was a kid.

We played stickball and dodgeball on Cooper Street. I went everywhere on roller skates. We had a favorite vacant lot around the corner where we played baseball. We left our doors open and unlocked day and night with no problems. Lots of kids played on Cooper Street, right in front of the house. The streets of Yonkers were filled with markets, pool halls, and bars. There were places where kids weren't allowed to go at night, where the toughs and the collar-up guys hung out on street corners and in back alleyways.

We lived walking distance from Yankee Stadium and from the Yonkers Raceway; my parents, Josie and Paul, earned a little extra pocket money charging people to park their cars in our driveway during baseball and horseracing season. Then my parents and their friends walked to the track to watch and bet on the trotters.

Yonkers had a wide range of neighborhoods representing the various immigrant groups, including Italian, German, Hungarian, Irish, Russian, and Austrian. It was a lot like New York City, which was about fifteen miles south of us. New Yorkers seemed the same all over. You couldn't tell if someone was from Yonkers or Mount Vernon—or the Bronx or Brooklyn, for that matter. This was the greaser era, as the doo-wop 1950s were coming to a close. I started out as a bit of a greaser myself. Hair slicked back with Vitalis. My sisters and I walked to school, two or three miles, even through the winter snows. The principals rarely closed the schools during the heaviest snowstorms. It would have to be a record-breaking blizzard for us to hear on the radio that school was shut down.

I remember Jack the truant officer. You kept your distance from him, otherwise that bastard would cross you, and I would get into huge trouble at home. But unlike most of my friends, I didn't play much hooky, although I was a mischievous kid. Didn't do well in school. I got whacked all the time in class. Corporal punishment was the norm both at home and at school.

I hid my report cards when I got home, but my mother or father would find them. Then I'd get the beating of my life. My parents didn't get too involved with my school; nor did they care much about my education or what was going on in my life. That is, until I did something wrong. Then I got another beating. For instance, when I did my homework with Mom or Dad, if I gave them a wrong answer, I'd get smacked in the face. I was scared to death. Damned if I did. Damned if I didn't. I'd be sitting there, struggling through my homework, crying after getting smacked, my lip bleeding. Then if I got hit when I didn't deserve it, my father, rather than saying he was sorry, would yell, "That's one for next time!"

My parents kept a real cat-o'-nine-tails around the house, and we got beaten with nine leather ends. Both Mom and Dad dished out the punishment. And my sisters got it, too. We took a few trips to the hospital. My mom didn't work. She was a stay-at-home mom. She had some long fat Italian wooden spoons she used to stir the gravy, and every so often, she'd break one over me. My mom sure knew how to push the old man's buttons. When he'd come walking into the house after a hard day's work, especially if she had a hard day with us, she knew just how to get him going. Then he'd give us a beating.

Like my grandfather, all my father did was work. Work was his whole life. He worked in home improvement once he married my mom. My father replaced windows and doors. When I was a kid, I went to work for him during the summer. We'd take doors and windows out of old buildings and put new ones in. I would get two cents a window and five cents a door. That's how I earned my pocket money. It was a tough living for my dad.

My father had his own business twice, and both times failed at it. He wasn't successful at anything he did, and he more or less depended on my grandfather to bail him out. At least that's how my mother saw things. There were difficulties because my mom resented my grandfather's hold on my father. She felt that my father could never be a man because he depended on his father. It was a touchy situation for our family having to rely so much on my grandfather. But if we didn't, we wouldn't have had a house to live in.

There was always a battle going on between my mother and my grandfather. When I was a kid, my sisters and I were forbidden to go down the block to visit my grandmother and grandfather's house. We'd sneak down there anyway, and my grandmother made apple pie for us. She would serve a slice of apple pie with a cup of coffee to my sister and me. Of course we'd get caught all the time, and that would piss off my mother no end.

My family practically invented the term *dysfunctional*. With the yelling going on, my home life was chaos. Lots and lots of screaming. The children didn't grow up particularly tight as brothers and sisters and didn't look out for each other. Since my grandfather had the money that my dad didn't, he paid the piper and called the tune, which only made things worse between my mom and dad. Since my mother *hated* my grandfather for the way he controlled his son, her husband, our home was a battlefield.

We kids were caught in the middle, as the frustrations my grandfather caused between my parents were passed down to us.

Actually, my father drank very little. He might have enjoyed a shot of whiskey or a beer every once in a while, but I never saw him drunk. My mother, like I said, was the heavy drinker. She was one of those closet drinkers who hid bottles of booze around the house. She drank whiskey. She didn't have a particular brand; she just drank whatever was available. I didn't see the bottles too often. They were stashed up in the cabinets. She would slug it down in the middle of the night, and then put it back up in the cabinet. She rarely left a bottle out on the table. Then once she got a buzz on, it was a horror show. She'd drink all night and fight with my dad, then sleep all day while the old man had to get up and go to work. Then *he'd* come home dead tired after staying up at night fighting with her.

Today I realize that my mom was truly a sick person, a closet drunk. She should have been treated for mental problems. Instead, she would take a Valium, and after she'd pop a little yellow pill, she would drink more. It was a vicious cycle. Then my father would come home and it was time for more rage.

It got so crazy, sometimes the cops would have to come out to the house. My earliest memory is being five years old, sitting on the floor with my sister. Both of us crying. What can you do, when you're that young, if your mother is trying to jump out the window while your father is screaming at her? Like I said, it was chaos.

Looking back, I was a lonely kid growing up. I knew nothing about nothing. Yonkers was a tough town to be raised in. People, including me, saw themselves as tough guys. But deep, deep, deep inside, I was a pretty scared kid, especially when Dad and Mom fought. I lived in fear of the two of them separating. Back then divorce was a mark of shame and instability among families. Something to be feared.

I remember my first drink. I was twelve years old. We were celebrating Easter over at my grandfather's house. Shots of whiskey were lined up on the table. It was just before mealtime and everybody was out of the house, so I downed a couple of shots, a lot for a kid my age. I was completely wasted. At first, it tasted awful, but I wound up doing it on a few more occasions. After a couple of times, I became a regular drinker, and once I adjusted to the buzz, I enjoyed it more.

As much as I didn't want it to happen, alcohol became a huge part of *my* family legacy, and when it's your turn to change it, unless you can get help, it's hard to break the chain.

Though he didn't drink, Dad was no positive role model. Other than working with a shovel, I wasn't encouraged to do anything interesting with my life. The only true role model I had was on my father's side: Uncle Emil. Emil Teutul was a heavy drinker and a gambler, but he was the one person in my life who spent time with me as a kid. He took an interest in me. If I had to get the yard cleaned, Uncle Emil would lend a hand. Emil was a tall, good-looking guy at six-foot-one. He was a ladies' man, and was married a few times. We lived in the same house together. Shared a bedroom.

Uncle Emil didn't drink when he was at home. He would go out and do that with his gambling friends. Emil was like a real buddy to me. The thing I remember most about Uncle Emil was that he was never pissed off at me. We'd build double-winger model airplanes together, World War I biplanes made of plastic or balsa wood. Then we'd hand-paint them together. I had a nice collection of model airplanes.

Emil got into car accidents all the time. He'd have glass in his eye and would be stitched up from one of his many car crashes. One night some bookies were chasing him, and he flipped the car over. He flew out of the car; the car landed on top of him, and he died instantly. Gone at the age of thirty-five. I remember my father getting the phone call real late at night and freaking out. I had never seen my father cry before. He was devastated. And so was I.

Emil was a special person in my life. Then he was gone. I got sick to my stomach and threw up when my parents told me what had happened. I was eight years old.

While hard work was ingrained in me, I didn't learn to love activities like sports until much later in my life. I never tried out for sports in school. To be into sports meant you needed discipline, which was something I saw myself as sorely lacking. Partly because of my tough family upbringing and my lack of success in school, I looked for love and encouragement elsewhere. That's when I became an animal lover.

As a kid, I always had a dog by my side. They were mostly raggedy dogs, but they gave me peace in my life. The dog that I remember best was a mutt named Shep. I called him Old Shep, just like the Elvis Presley song. Shep was my buddy, but after I went away for a few days, he got killed. Dogs roamed free around Yonkers, chasing cars and delivery trucks. He must have gotten run over, although for years I looked around for Shep, thinking he might show up. That's the way I am today with my dogs, especially Gus, whose face is tattooed on my arm. I love dogs. I love animals. And they love me. They're my sole source of unconditional love. When Shep and my uncle Emil died, so did the two best parts of my childhood.

At some point, things were getting a little too crazy between my grandparents and my mom. My mom felt like a prisoner in my grandfather's house. So she kept bugging my father to move the hell out of Yonkers. In 1961, when I was twelve, my family moved to Rockland County, an hour outside the city. Rockland County was much more rural, more countrified, and a lot cheaper. We wound up buying a house in Muncie, New York. Later we lost the house in Muncie and moved on to an apartment in Spring Valley. I got us thrown out of there for breaking the washing machine, stealing money from the soda machines, and smashing windows in the building we lived in. After that, we settled down in a village called Pearl River.

There was no escaping my grandfather. We lived in a fixer-upper in Pearl River that he had bought for my father. So my grandfather came up and saw us every weekend. When there was no work to be done around the house, he would toss me a pick and shovel.

"Dig a trench all the way around the house. Tar it. Mix the concrete. Pour it and fill it in."

I had to have a pick and shovel in my hands to stay on my grandfather's good side. Once we moved to Pearl River, I was living in the boondocks. We had a convent behind our house, and beyond that, woods. I would venture into the woods for hours, from dusk until dawn, hunting with a bow and arrow.

I was just out of grammar school, a skinny, weedy kid. Being the new kid in junior high, I got beat up a lot. When I was fourteen years old, one of the school bullies worked me over bad. That was it. I'd had enough. I responded by building a wooden bench down in the basement. Then I got a cheap set of weights. I ate brewer's yeast and hoisted a set of old plastic free weights filled with sand. Every day after school, I'd run down to the basement by myself and work out. Hard. I worked out until I puked. But in four or five months' time, I stacked on about forty pounds of muscle. I was skinny no more.

I wasn't much of a student in high school. I was lousy in math, science, and English. So I became Shop Guy. You know the type. By my senior year, I took three shop classes so I could graduate. Metal. Wood. Auto. By then, I was good in gym and PE. I was now strong as an ox and had good coordination. I could do gymnastics, but I wouldn't play sports. Although I had the build, I didn't try out for football. Instead, I signed up for welding classes, spending half my school day at a nearby trade school.

Upon graduation, the kids at my high school were glad to see the back of me. Nobody suspected I'd amount to much of anything because I had no real aspirations. My next-door neighbor was a New York City cop, so I took the entrance test. Twice. Failed it both times. The test was tough, fifteen pages long. I flunked the second exam by one point. I was one point away from being a New York City cop, and that might have been the end of this story. But the times were a-changing.

The 1960s counterculture scene hit me before I left high school. I experimented with pot and started listening to psychedelic rock and roll. The Vietnam War was in full swing. I thought I might get drafted. I had a couple of friends in the merchant marine, and they were making good money. So after I graduated in 1967, I decided to join up and go out to sea.

What the hell, I thought. I had no prospects, and I knew a guy who could get me in. I was eighteen years old, and a stint in the merchant qualified as military service. So I enlisted and began serving my hitch right around Christmas 1967, after I left high school. They sent me to Piney Point, Maryland, where I completed a twelve-week class, similar to boot camp. They promised I'd sail around the world, and they weren't kidding. I hopped on an old 1942 Enid Victory ship filled with ammunition and supplies, and we sailed off to Vietnam to deliver ammo to the troops.

Hard work followed me out to sea. My responsibilities included painting and scraping and scrubbing the deck. At night, I'd keep watch. It was a great opportunity. For our first stop, we docked in Panama, where you could buy Panama Red, supposedly the best grass in the world. You could get high on the ship and nobody knew. Once we landed in Panama, we scored a large bag with weed filled up to the top. We rolled enormous joints six inches long. The first time we smoked it—and I had smoked pot for years—I was getting ready to go out on watch. I was supposed to stand out in the bow and look for other ships. But after I smoked that joint, I got so messed up, I thought I was tripping. The watch commander was looking for me to start my shift. He came in and out of my room, asking where I had gone. I was so paranoid and buzzed on Panama Red, I had hidden underneath my bunk.

The mothball Enid was so old, she kept breaking down. We sailed out of Panama to Hawaii. Then over to the Philippines and then on to Vietnam. On our way from the Philippines back to Hawaii, we broke down in the middle of the Pacific Ocean. We lost power—no electricity, no lights, no nothing. Dead in the water. A tugboat had to bring us in. It took two whole weeks for it to tow us back into Hawaii, and it was party time again once we hit Honolulu.

I finished a nine-month tour, and that was it. I'd planned to go right back out, but when I got home, my friends were wearing bell-bottoms and long hair. I pulled a high number on the draft lottery. Had I not, I could have continued sailing with the merchant marine. My option was to sail another three to six months a year, which would have been considered my military duty. But Woodstock had already happened in 1969, just as I returned home from sea. And by 1970, the Vietnam War was winding down. Culturally, I was out of the loop. But I grew a beard and long hair. I smoked a lot of pot. Dropped acid. I dug the drug scene and especially enjoyed the whole free-love thing. But I didn't consider myself a hippie. I was the rowdy guy. A drinker. A hell-raiser. While the whole hippie thing was good for picking up chicks, I'd much rather be drinking a bottle of whiskey and getting into a barroom fight than preaching peace and love.

In 1970, I settled down (a little) and moved back to Rockland County and Pearl River. By then, I'd picked up on welding and fixing cars. Not sure what to do with my life, I fell deeply in love with a raven-haired girl named Marcy. She was Lebanese, a very exotic beauty. Lost in her long black hair, I fell madly in love with her. But she gave me the heave-ho. I was so heartbroken that my mother and father worried about me. That's how brokenhearted I was. She was my first love, and I fell hard.

Still, things worked out for the better. I called on another girl whom I'd been sweet on back when we were both in high school. Her name was Paula Leonardo. She was Italian, just like my mom. I thought she was pretty, and during high school I'd tried to call her. But she wouldn't give me the time of day. After we both graduated, before I took off to sea and she went off to college, we spent a little time together. Despite my family experiences, I believed in marriage. My parents, as miserable as they were, and as much as they hated each other, stayed together until my mother died of cirrhosis of the liver in 1978. I grew up with a dominant mother. She ruled over my father, which was degrading to him *and* to me. I vowed my own family life would be different.

I guess I charmed Paula enough that after a couple of years out of the merchant marine and on my own, we got married in 1972, when we were both twenty-three. It was time to figure out what to do with my life. I was anxious to start a family. But throughout my days growing up, I was convinced I was a loser and was sure I would never amount to anything. Parents. Teachers. Principals. They wrote me off. Loser. Loser. Loser. But now that I was married, I had it etched in my mind. I would set out to prove them wrong.

Two smiling faces: Paul Sr., a proud new papa with Paul Michael, his firstborn son. (Photo: Paula Teutul personal collection)

CHAPTER 3

DAYS OF IRON AND STEEL

SENIOR:

Call me a late bloomer. I didn't start riding motorcycles until I hit my twenties. Unlike guys like Vinnie DiMartino and Rick Petko, two of our skilled builders and fabricators at OCC, I wasn't riding motorcycles as a little kid. Back in the day, there weren't a lot of bike riders in my neighborhoods. Bikes were rare creatures.

Like so many of my generation, my earliest recollection of becoming interested in motorcycles came when the movie *Easy Rider* hit the theaters in 1969. I had returned to Rockland County from being out at sea. There was something about that movie. After I saw *Easy Rider,* I dreamed of one day building a bike of my own and riding it around the world.

But first, it was time to settle down and make a living. After Paula and I married in 1972, I more or less picked up from where I'd left off. I messed around for a few years. I had a few jobs. Nothing steady. Then I found a job close to New York City with Metropolitan Tobacco, driving a truck delivering candy and cigarettes to bars and liquor stores. During this time, my drinking escalated. Just like my days out at sea, I was able to keep a whiskey buzz going while finishing up my daily delivery routes.

It was around this time I rode my first motorcycle. A buddy of mine had a Honda 175 with ape hangers on it. It was a funny little thing. He picked me up on it one day in front of my house. We were riding down the road, and then he asked, "Wanna ride?"

"Sure."

He pulled over and gave me a quick lesson. I didn't need much instruction. I got on the seat and rode down Middletown Road. It was my very first experience on a bike. I was hooked like a dog from that day on. Not long after that, I picked up a used motorcycle. I rode it around for a year. A 1971 Triumph. Gold and black with streaks of white in it.

While a Triumph is different from a Harley-Davidson, it was a notch or so above a Honda or a Yamaha. Harleys were damn expensive in those days. During the late 1960s and early '70s, most of the choppers I saw were cut from Triumphs. A Triumph motor had a fairly hearty sound to it. It didn't whine like a lawn mower the way the Japanese bikes did. There were other limey bikes like Nortons and BSAs, but since I couldn't afford a Harley, I settled for the Triumph for two reasons. Number one, nobody made fun of them or of me for riding one. Number two, the Triumph was a fast friggin' bike. It had a decent sound to it. Handled well. Set me back nine hundred bucks, but it was only one year old. Not a bad deal, and much less than the twenty-four hundred dollars I later paid for my first Harley, which, while considered big dough back then, doesn't compare with today's prices.

I rode that Triumph mostly back and forth to work. On the weekends, I'd venture upstate on a few rides. I hardly did any long-distance or cross-country riding. Upstate New York was enough of an escape. I loved getting away. I still do.

At the time I bought the Triumph, I didn't know what I was doing with my life. Didn't know what I was going to be if and when I grew up. Luckily, the welding and shop courses I took in high school came in handy. I wound up getting a job with my brother-in-law. He had his own welding shop. I worked for him for about nine months before he went out of business. After that, I bounced around a few of the local Rockland County shops. It was the same old crap.

Then I realized three important things about myself.

First, I could never be the guy who worked and took orders from the boss. Working for the man had its disadvantages. I didn't like how I was treated working for other people, and if I felt looked down upon, tough luck. I found that unacceptable. I needed to be my own boss.

Second, I've always considered myself a risk-taker. So I decided to start my own welding business, working with iron and steel.

Third, and most important: If I could have people working for me, I wanted to give them opportunities that nobody'd ever offered me. Although I can be a hothead and a taskmaster (just like my grandfather), I was determined to treat my fellow workers fairly and with dignity. While I'm hardest on my sons (just like my grandfather), I treated my people fairly. Right from the start, I wanted to be thought of as a tough but fair boss. That's been a priority. You're only as good as the people around you. Your people make you and break you. So you'd better treat them right. Ultimately, I'm the one in charge; I'm the guy at the top of the responsibility ladder. But the bottom line is, I try to treat people the way I would like to be treated. Do unto others. The Golden Rule. That's not the modern corporate way today, but in my businesses, it's been that way. And I wouldn't have it any other way.

So I bought myself a truck and some welding gear and started out doing odd jobs working for myself. I'd build exhaust systems and stuff like that. I did that for a little while, and things were okay. I was picking up jobs here and there. Then I met a guy named Bill Belmonte. Bill was a jobber: If you had a shop, he'd steer work your way. He had several deals going with a string of other shops, doing work for him. He advised me to expand beyond my truck and welding gear, to go get a shop, and he'd keep me busy. For instance, he'd get me work making wrought-iron railings; I could charge seven dollars a foot to make and install them. Then he'd take a 10 percent commission.

I flashed on a guy I'd met who also worked for my brother-in-law. Fred Gerini came from Brooklyn. He was a smart guy. He had a college education. He went to school for steel fabrication. Me, I could outwork anybody, but Fred had smarts. Together, I figured we'd make a good team. So I called Freddy and proposed taking a shot at becoming partners. Make a go of it in Rockland County.

Bill the jobber had other ideas. He urged me to move a little farther north, into Orange County. That's what led us to Middletown in the Hudson Valley near the village of Montgomery and the small town of Newburgh. By 1973, Fred and I started up P&F Ironworks. Soon the work came in and we were cruising along nicely.

In addition to knowing the steel biz, Fred was a motorcycle freak, a real Harley guy. Plus, he could build a bike from the ground up. Fred used to say, the thing about a motorcycle is that it has to have the right lines. It has to have a look and a flow. Anything that disrupts the flow, once it breaks the line of the bike, it's gotta go. I learned that early on. I've had a good eye, even in the steel business. I never needed to use a level. I could eyeball a beam and immediately tell you whether or not it was straight. I think you need that same precise eye to build cycles. Being around Fred, I watched him stretch frames and build up every part of the bike. Before I could afford to buy an extended Springer for a chopper, I'd watch Fred improvise by building a jig using Ford radius rods out of the old hot rods, because they were tapered the same as a Springer on a Harley. He'd stretch the Springers, stretch the frame, kick the neck out to rake it, then take that Springer front end and add the radius rods to make the bike whatever length he wanted. Because you couldn't buy parts at that time, you had to make them yourself. And everything had to be straight.

Right around the time we started the steel business, I decided to sell the Triumph and buy my first Harley. I picked out a brand-new 1974 Harley, an AMF-made model. I got the bug and started getting involved in bikes. My wife didn't ride much on the back of my motorcycles. She wasn't into it, but riding gave me a feeling of coolness, that *look-at-me* feeling of respectability that I craved.

I'd learned from Fred that a motorcycle was more than something you ride from point A to point B. Now it had to be sculptured, refined, customized, and chopped. I needed to transform my bike into something more personal. And I found out that the process never ends.

My '74 Harley was a Superglide. A narrow glide. It wasn't a really expensive model. It had a turtle tank that said AMF on it. At first I liked the AMF Harleys, but now I don't. My experience with the '74 Harley showed that bad workmanship was commonplace, and the bike slung oil. During that period, there were rumors that Harley-Davidson workers sabotaged the bikes on the assembly line. I was shocked to find a crushed cigarette packet stuck inside the oil tank of a bike I worked on. Plus, I'm not that crazy about the designs back then. I don't like the half tanks. So I did a whole transformation on that Superglide. I was always changing stuff on it. One year, I just took it apart and cut the frame, stretched it out, added four inches onto the lower legs, and, vroom, it became my first chopper. And I did it myself at the steel shop.

Actually, that Superglide might be considered more of a bobber than a chopper. My bobber wasn't as stretched out as a chopper. It was more like a stripped-down version of a Harley. I changed the oil tank. I cut the fenders. I had the fender built and mounted right to the swing arm. I put a special set of shocks on there.

I went with the drag-bar look, with ape hangers, at first. To me, there's nothing more comfortable. It had nothing to do with the look. People think ape hangers are uncomfortable, but when you're riding, the hanging position is comfortable for me. It's easier to handle. Whether or not they're legal depends on the height of the bars. They keep changing the laws in New York. And the cops keep an eye on you.

My first AMF became a cool bike. It had a slick paint job—bright red with a smiling picture of the sun on the tank. Remember that sun face on the old box of Kellogg's Corn Flakes? Kinda like that. Then the red paint job broke out into a yellow flame. I sent it out west to Minneapolis to get painted by a guy named Kenny Winters. I had it pin-striped, too. Back then, there were only a few good painters who were specialists. We had a guy in Orange County in the early days called Joe the Beatnik. He was The Man, too. Unfortunately, there weren't a lot of places to go for bike parts. Ted's V-Twin in Newburgh. Ted had a garage that I would go to on a Saturday. That's where everybody went in our area. He had motorcycle parts hanging high, on shelves and from the ceiling, and he was one of the biggest distributors in the area. His place was almost two blocks long.

I took a real chance cutting the frame on my first Harley, but I didn't care. Back then, it was an exciting challenge. I now had a chopped-out bike that I'd done myself. It was new. Exciting. A special source of pride. I named it the Sunshine Bike. I felt as great about myself as I did that bike. I had started something, followed through, and finished it. I still own that motorcycle, and it sits proudly in my private collection.

When I first chopped that '74 bike, it was during a time when there weren't a lot of custom bikes around. I experienced an unbelievable feeling of joy riding that chopper. It was indescribable. I felt like such a renegade. I truly stuck out on the road, cruising on a glide ride like that. Like *Easy Rider.*

From the mid-1960s through the early '70s became the golden era of the chopper. Like the David Mann paintings and illustrations in *Easyriders.* Like the Hell's Angels' image. Real chopper influences. And back then, Harley wasn't too happy about people chopping up their bikes. Later in the 1970s, when the times started changing, East Coast choppers were getting more acceptable.

Then after the mid-1970s, choppers started to fade out of fashion and didn't rebound until the late '90s. But still, I loved a timeless David Mann–style bike. Today there are so many different versions and looks of choppers. The bobbed fender. The flat fender. The Springer. The Indian. Wide glide. Narrow glide. You could change them around and they'd have a classic look about them.

Choppers from the '70s were difficult to ride. No front brakes. Only a disc brake in the back. We ran a small wheel in the front—the Springer front ends way out there—and if your geometry wasn't exact, the wheels would wobble. Plus, they were dangerous to maneuver. You had to pay attention.

Personally, I wasn't into riding with a group, let alone a patch-wearing, colors-flying motorcycle club. I'm not exactly what you'd call a joiner. I prefer riding by myself. If I want to ride slow, I ride slow. If I want to cruise fast, I kick it. While I'm not crazy about riding in a pack, occasionally I'll get out with ten or fifteen guys, and we'll go out riding. But generally I ride alone.

About a year after we opened P&F Ironworks (named for Paul and Fred), I was working overtime in the shop one night building some wrought-iron railings. Inside, we had a large paint tank. After I made the railings, I'd dip them in thick enamel paint and hang them up to dry. Anyway, I was working by myself, getting ready for the paint dip process. The tank was full and I was over at the workbench grinding when a spark hit the tank. The paint tank immediately burst into flames. Underneath the tank were five more one-gallon pails of paint. Within a matter of minutes, they exploded. In about three hours, the entire building burned to the ground. I had lost everything. With only a pittance of insurance money, P&F Ironworks was virtually eliminated.

I had no place to go.

Then out of the blue, another crazy thing happened. At the time, my partner, Fred, had a girlfriend who was a devout Christian. Almost overnight, Fred went from a crazy Brooklyn bike rider to a born-again Christian. Next thing I knew, he had a Bible in his hand. I didn't mind that he was born again until he started preaching to me. After the shop burned down, our relationship fell apart. Then Fred wanted out of the business.

After Fred bailed, I salvaged whatever tools I could from the fire and began working out of my garage. I had a few leftover accounts, including a big housing development that I was doing railings for. I was back to working alone. But I wasn't down long. I decided to bring in a second partner, Johnny Grasso, another guy I'd worked with at my brother-in-law's shop. The neighbors and my wife were tired of me running my business from home. I figured I couldn't get away with it much longer, so I opened a new shop in the tiny nearby village of Montgomery with Johnny. We called it Paul's Welding.

During my start-up days in the Ironworks business, my drinking escalated, getting more and more out of control. Through it all, I managed to show up to work every day. My poison was Black Velvet, the brand on the buses and billboards with the smooth sexy girl in the black velvet evening dress. Whenever I entered a crowded bar and started drinking, the bartender would invariably slide the Black Velvet bottle in front of me.

"Here, son, keep track on your own."

I became the legendary drinker of Orange County. I would start with shots, and then rarely stop. With a single beer chaser, I could drink down an entire quart of whiskey. During one lunch break, I stood at the bar drinking for two straight hours. When I got up to leave, the bartender called me back over.

"Hey listen, pal, do me a favor. The next time you come in here, let me know and I'll hire another bartender."

My partner, Johnny, was a drinker like me. We were stone-cold alco-worka-holics. We busted ass, then spent the remainder of the day in the bar. We worked hard and drank harder. I developed an ultrahigh tolerance for alcohol fueled by a relentless work ethic. I drank heavily, humped iron all day long, and ran up and down tall ladders, carrying huge steel beams on my back. It's what I had to do to survive.

I soon became an insane neurotic living on the edge. My family life and my work became two separate realities. On the drinking side, the wilder the men and women I hung out with, the better. I loved the action of knocking back a few bottles a day, hanging out with people who weren't exactly what you would call responsible.

On the other hand, I felt that if I was going to raise a family, I needed a wife who was the opposite of my wild and irresponsible self. That woman was Paula Leonardo. My obsessive work ethic of over sixty hours a week at the shop coupled with nonstop drinking would soon take its toll on Paula, me, and our newborn son, Paul Michael Teutul, who entered the world on October 2, 1974. With two conflicting lifestyles, I was headed on a serious collision course, with the worst yet to come.

CHAPTER

The famed Sunshine Bike, Senior's first Harley, followed him through the several phases of his life, not to mention numerous thrills, chills, and spills on the road. That's why the bike remains in the family. (Photo: OCC Archives)

THRILLS AND SPILLS AND DRUGS AND BOOZE

SENIOR:

I could tell you not to drink or take drugs until I'm blue in the face, but no amount of preaching will make you stop unless you're ready and willing. So in the interests of disclosure, here are a few examples of the insanity I went through as a slave to alcohol and drugs.

I've always been the risk-taker, the guy who, if we agreed to jump off a bridge, would be the first to leap. Throw that television through the window? Don't ask me a second time. It's going through the window. The cars we drove, the bikes we rode, the drinks we drank, the drugs we took, and everything had to be maximum crazy. There was no middle ground. Only extremes for me. I learned quickly that you do a lot of crazy things when you're drinking. I've had my employees by the throat, throwing them down a flight of stairs. An hour later, we've got our arms around each other, drunk off our asses. I started drinking when I was twelve. By the time I returned from the merchant marine, I was a full-blown alcoholic.

I'll bet I must have totaled at least twenty cars in my life. Once I totaled two cars in a week. One happened when I was driving home. Of course I was drinking. My next-door neighbor was having a graduation party when I drove onto her freakin' yard. Once I got back on the road, I drove down the street, unaware of what I'd just done.

So I leapt out of the car and took a long piss. Next thing I knew, the cops slipped the cuffs on me and I was on my way to jail. I got lucky. I'd only spent time in the drunk tank a few times. Most of the time I squeaked by. Plus, back in the day, they rarely messed with you about drinking and driving. Today, forget about it. You'll go directly to jail and experience all the headaches of having your car impounded, paying the legal fees and fines, the rising car insurance rates—not to mention the danger of hurting or killing someone. I got in just as much trouble riding motorcycles as I did driving automobiles. I'll give you a couple of examples of close calls. Three, in fact.

The first one was on my very first bike, the Triumph. It was my first time riding in the rain. I was going down a hill when a lady in front of me decided to make a left-hand turn. As I hit her, my leg got caught in the front of her car while the Triumph slid out from underneath me. I was barely able to grab the sissy bar and keep the bike up. That wasn't so bad.

A second crash was more serious. It happened on the '74 Harley Sunshine. I've been to hell and back on that bike, which is why I still own it. My '74 was brand new at the time, and again, these were my drinking days. It was during the five o'clock rush hour. I was pretty blitzed when I pulled onto the Palisades Parkway. I was looking down at my speedometer because, on a brand-new bike, you're not supposed to ride it too fast during the break-in period. I watched the speedometer closely as I brought up each gear on the bike. But when I looked up, there was a lady in a car stopped dead in front of me. I had only a split second to react. My first instinct was to hit the car and slide over the top. A fraction of a second later, I tried going around the back of the car. My front tire hit her rear tire. While the bike slid, I found myself soaring over the middle of the parkway, the bike sliding as I was airborne.

I came down hard on my shoulder, bounced back up, and spun around. All the time Sunshine was behind me. We wound up on the grass median, between the north- and southbound traffic, with Sunshine next to me, not a yard away. I looked up. Miraculously, I was alive.

What had happened was this: When the first car stopped and I looped around it, a guy in another lane nearly ran me over. But I didn't know that. So when I bounced onto the median, he pulled over, too. The guy was shaking like a leaf, freaking out, wondering if I was okay or if I was even alive. I stood up, looking over my bike. I was drunk.

"Just a second," I told him. The impact of the crash hadn't fazed me. I surveyed the damage. My fender was bent in, and the shifter was bent. The guy was yapping away, wanting to know if I was hurt.

"Do you have any tools on you?" I asked.

Fortunately, he had a toolbox in the back of his car. So I took his hammer and pulled the shifter out, kicked the bike, and, boom, it started right up. I told the guy, "Thanks a lot," got back on my Sunshine, and rode home. Later that night, I went on another drinking binge.

The third spill also involved my '74, after I customized it. There was nobody home at my place when I started drinking glasses of vodka. I liked to get a quick buzz on, so I poured four eight-ounce glasses of vodka and quickly downed them all. Then I jumped on Sunshine. I loved riding like that. I shudder to think about the danger I put people through, not to mention myself, on the road drunk as a skunk.

At some point, I wound up meeting up with friends who had scored some quality weed. Stoned out of my gourd on top of my vodka buzz, on my way home, about a quarter of a mile shy of my house, it occurred to me that I was riding on the wrong side of the road. Coming up over a blind spot, I met an oncoming car. I swerved to the right and hit a tree stump. I must have flown about fifteen or twenty feet before I hit another tree head-on. The impact cracked the helmet off my head and knocked me out cold. I got quickly back up, but found that I'd lost my memory. I was sitting by the side of the road when one of my neighbors drove by and spotted me. Since I didn't know my own name, he threw my bike into the back of his pickup and drove me home.

When I got home, I couldn't remember who I was, which freaked me out. So for some reason, I took off my clothes. By this time, people were coming to the door to check up on me, to see if I was okay. Unfortunately, I answered the door wearing nothing but my helmet. The accident literally knocked the sense out of me. Although they took me to the hospital, I went to work the next day. I didn't know what a concussion was. It took me a year or better to get back to full strength after that one.

My wife didn't notice my abusive drinking when we first got married, because drinking was a much more acceptable vice back then. Everybody was young and having a good time boozing. At age sixteen, we knew which bars would serve us. It only took a couple of years for me to realize that my excessive drinking wasn't just a youthful phase I was going through, and that I wasn't going to stop anytime soon.

Paula kept a closer eye on my drinking. At least she tried to. On a Sunday, for instance, while trying to keep me inside the house, I figured out the best way to cop a buzz.

"I'm going down to get a pack of cigarettes," I assured Paula. "Be back in a few."

From the time I left my house to the time I got back home, I might have been gone fifteen or twenty minutes, tops. I'd gone straight down to the bar where everybody knew me, walked inside, ordered a dozen shots, and downed them in record time: five, ten minutes. Boom. Boom. Boom. Boom. When I came home and assumed the telltale position in my easy chair, Paula couldn't figure out how I'd managed to cop a buzz.

I was so out of hand, we couldn't keep booze around the house, except when I once threw a party. I bought gallons and gallons of every variety of liquor you could imagine. During the party, everyone drank beer. Nobody touched the liquor, leaving me with a closetful of half-gallon bottles of booze. I put the liquor in the downstairs closet, then ran up and down the stairs every chance I got to down a quick shot or three. Just like my mom. Normally, as I mentioned, I drank Black Velvet whiskey, but downstairs there was a closetful of vodka, gin, and scotch. I drank every single bottle dry. One day while looking down in the closet, Paula asked me what happened to the booze.

"It must have evaporated," I told her with a straight face.

I started smoking pot in high school, driving around with a few of my friends. I was in the tenth grade. After smoking it for the first time, while I sat inside my buddy's car, every time I moved my head around, it felt as if I was inside one of those glass snow globes that you shake at Christmas. This was when pot was quite the taboo drug, as serious as cocaine is now. Only beatniks and jazz musicians smoked pot back then. If you got caught with pot, it was a major crime. I had friends in Rockland County who got caught with a few joints doing five years in jail.

I smoked pot almost every day until I had to stop. The mix of alcohol and pot was spooking me. Sometimes I'd smoke a joint and wind up in somebody's house or wake up in a strange bedroom, not knowing how I got there.

I first took LSD two days after I got out of the merchant marine. I was riding in a car with five friends I had gone to school with. We were driving down to Jones Beach. Three of the guys had already dropped a hit of acid each, but I was too scared. The fourth guy was a real BS artist and a storyteller. He was ready to take his hit. But as he was talking away, I snatched the tab out of his hand and popped it into my mouth. I laughed nonstop for thirteen hours. On acid, everything seemed hilarious.

I did loads of mushrooms. Mescaline was my favorite. While most people used it for scientific or spiritual reasons, I took it just to go nuts. The next day, I couldn't talk because my jaws hurt from so much laughing.

One time a buddy and I took a hit of mescaline and walked into a nightclub. After we decided to leave, we couldn't find our way out of the club. When we'd finally made it out the door, we jumped into the car and drove down the parkway. I drove up a wall, cracked my distributor, and killed the engine. We got out, abandoned the car, and walked to the nearest phone booth. We were ten miles from my house, so I called a friend to ask him to come pick us up. Except when he asked us where we were, we couldn't figure it out. We spent the night sleeping along the parkway.

I did a lot of speed in my late twenties, mostly after the merchant marine. It gave me energy, or so I thought. Since I was drinking around the clock, I'd get up in the morning and pop a speed pill to make it to work. One day a friend of mine broke into a house and stole six pounds of pot, three pounds of hash, and a giant bag of pharmaceutical speed. I kept the entire bag of speed for myself, and did the whole bag. It lasted me eight months, my steady everyday supply. I mostly took it while I was working for my brother-in-law.

I admit I was a real garbage head. I did every drug. I was the guy who would walk into your house, open up your medicine cabinet, and pop three or four different pills at one time. I chugalugged cough syrup. The hardest stuff I tried was cocaine, which fortunately I didn't like. I only used it occasionally as a pick-me-up when I drank.

Toward the end of my drinking days, I seriously considered switching over to heroin. At the time, alcohol was tearing me up, eating me alive, so I figured heroin wouldn't screw up my system as badly. That was typical stupid drug-addict logic. Besides, I knew guys who did heroin, and one of them almost had me doing it. Thankfully, at the last minute, I came to my senses and backed off before falling down that cliff.

The scariest thought—one that haunts me to this day—is that I barely missed out on crack. Crack only became popular after I stopped drinking. Thank God. Crack surely would have killed me, because the percentage of addicts who stay off crack is nearly zero. That's because crack users are constantly chasing a cheap high that lasts only a few minutes. So you keep on using until you're broke, and then you die.

Another drug that rocked my socks was angel dust. Man, that stuff was too shameful even for me. I smoked it once, and at first, it seemed great. Then I bought an ounce of it, smoked it a second time, called up the guy I got it from, and gave it back to him. Bad, bad stuff. I was twenty-three at the time, dating my wife. That first time I tried angel dust was at a wedding with Paula's relatives. I was drinking heavily, so I took a hit of speed. I was already whacked on speed and alcohol when a cousin offered me a hit off his joint with angel dust mixed in.

After smoking it, on my way back to the wedding reception, I threw up all over myself. I hadn't realized I'd done it, and frankly, I couldn't have given a damn, that's how whacked out I was. Back inside the reception, everybody was dancing. Paula's uncles and aunts were there. I sat in a chair near the middle of the dance floor with puke all over my pants and shoes, and I didn't know it. I was so messed up that I left my car at Paula's house. The next day, I woke up high at four in the morning. I got dressed and walked the mile or so back to Paula's, knocked on the door, and asked her mother, "Is breakfast ready?"

As you can see, I was completely out of my tree, out of control, except for the control that drugs and alcohol held over my life. I'm not proud of the use and abuse I put my mind and body through. But at the same time, you've got to hit rock bottom before you can find the will to bounce back toward the top. I was closing in on the bottom when I decided to change course.

Paul Sr. assumes the telltale position, probably loaded, in his favorite easy chair during the early days of his family. (Photo: Paula Teutul personal collection)

CHAPTER 5

I'LL DRINK TOMORROW

SENIOR:

Just because my mother drank, did that necessarily mean I had to? Was alcoholism passed on through the family genes? These were questions I asked myself. And while I suspected alcoholism could be a physiological trait handed down through the family, was I destined to remain a hopeless, full-blown, brought-down-to-my-knees alcoholic?

I remember sitting in a room with my wife, Paula, feeling so helpless, like I had no control over my own life. I was dying, not because I was ill, but because I chose to die. I didn't want to drink anymore, but it was like being stuck in the pits of hell. I was physically, mentally, and spiritually stripped down to nothing but the need to get high. I didn't *want* to get high. I *needed* to get high. I no longer had a choice or a say. It was get high or die, and when you're in the throes of such helplessness, because you've spent years failing to beat it, at some point you just surrender to it. Your only alternative is to end it by dying. So I chose death. I remember sitting at the table with my wife in 1984, telling her I didn't want to die, but I was going to.

I knew about the 12 steps. My wife had entered a program for victims of alcoholism and had already attended five or six *years* of meetings. Living with me was driving her crazy—so crazy that my poor wife suffered a breakdown. She nearly lost her mind living with me. I was that crazy and far-gone.

So it was decided that I would go into rehab. At the time, about all I had left was my reputation as a drinker. Everybody knew me by how much I drank. The guys who worked for me at the Ironworks drank the way I drank. Every day, we went through the same routine. Go to work. Three o'clock. Go get the whiskey. Or else I might sit down and drink a quart of whiskey for lunch, go back to work, then come back at five o'clock and drink another quart of whiskey, *then* drive home. And I did that constantly.

On the day I was to leave for rehab, I popped six Valiums, drank half a gallon of wine, and chased that down with a pint of cognac. Then I decided against rehab. I knew I was taking a chance not going in. But I enjoyed living on the edge. I still do. I wanted to take the risk by going in a different direction.

Most of my family wanted me to enter rehab. But rehab sounded like just another broken promise. Still, my situation was critical. I could see death coming. You know when your body is deteriorating. I was throwing up blood. So when I got up on the morning of January 7, 1985, and went to work, I said to myself, *I'm going to a 12-step meeting instead.* I'd gone once or twice before, drunk. But this time, I thought, *Screw this. I'll go to a meeting.*

My main objection to rehab was rooted in my work ethic. As small a business as I had going at the time, it was something I couldn't just walk away from. I couldn't be away for a whole month. So instead, I chose to attend a 12-step meeting secretly because I knew that if I told any of the guys at work I'd stopped drinking, they wouldn't take me seriously. I had enough trouble taking myself seriously. We'd heard a hundred times before how I wasn't going to drink anymore.

So I went to the meeting. And after the first one, I went to another. Then another. Then another. How I hated it. I didn't say one word at those meetings. I never talked to a single soul. Nobody talked to me. Nobody came near. Then pretty soon, I started seeing a pattern. As long as I attended those meetings, I didn't drink. So another day and another meeting went by. And then another. No drinking.

During the day, I was working with the guys. We're out on a job. It's three o'clock and they're sending me out to go get the booze. As we're riding back from the job site, they're slugging down shots of whiskey while I'm sitting in the truck, dry. Believe me, that was the hardest thing I had to do in my life. There was nothing more I wanted to do than, oh my God, join in and get drunk. But I kept right on going to meetings instead, until the next thing I knew, a month went by. Then at one of my meetings, someone said, "Today. Just don't drink today."

What the hell, I thought. *Just don't drink today.* That made sense. Sounded easy. But it wasn't. So instead I told myself, *I'll drink tomorrow.* The promise of not drinking today but drinking tomorrow actually relieved the tension and got me through the roughest part, my first month of sobriety.

At work it was the same old dance: Let's drink! I hadn't told anybody I'd quit. I was supposedly taking a break. *I'll drink tomorrow,* I kept telling myself. But I didn't.

Next thing I knew, six months passed! Then eight months. Then ten months. Then a whole freakin' year went by, and believe me, it took a full year just to blow the cobwebs out of my brain. When you live your life as an addict or an alcoholic, you surround yourself with the wrong people and you no longer know what the norm is. And besides, you hate the norm. If, for example, someone didn't drink, you felt you couldn't trust him because he was being normal. The enemy.

The next thing I learned was through my sponsor. *I now had choices.* Before, I felt I had no choice; only death. Now I started making subtle choices and changes in my environment. The insurance people warned me that we couldn't drink at the shop anymore. So I initiated a few rules. All the while, throughout the first two or three years, I didn't miss a single meeting. Every night for nine years straight, I attended meetings around town. The final phase came when I was invited to speak. Then there was the counseling. Ten years of counseling. Family counseling. Marriage counseling. One-on-one counseling. I became the King of Counseling. Through my sobriety, I was reaching out to my family to make up for the times I hadn't been there, physically and mentally.

It was through the grace of God that sobriety sneaked up on me. Otherwise I may have self-destructed. But instead, I felt the power of God *gradually* lead me to abandon the drink and the drugs. The reason the 12-step program worked for me was that it was a gradual program, not a one-step overnight thing. One day at a time. One step at a time. *I'll drink tomorrow,* I told myself. But I stopped wanting to, so I never did.

I have my coins (recovery anniversary medallions) to this day, although I haven't been to a meeting in over ten years. My goal is to learn to live life on life's terms. Some people need to go to meetings for the rest of their lives. For me, the 12-step program's main purpose was to put me in a position where I can live my life and not use meetings as a crutch.

Part of getting sober was a matter of substitution. Two years after I got straight, I built my own gym equipment, filling my basement and garage with iron. I started working out again, getting stronger and stronger. So far I've been working out for eighteen years, and while I can bench 455 pounds, I still aggressively challenge myself. Yes, it's another compulsion and possibly an addiction, but it's a helluva lot better (and cheaper) addiction than drinking whiskey and smoking pot.

What makes me such an aggressive person today is that I've always been told that I was a loser and would never amount to anything. That's partly what drove me and what kept me going through the fire, the drink, and the drugs. That and not giving up. I never once stopped trying. I was determined to break through. A lot of terrible things happened to me that should have shut me down a hundred times. But never once did I consider quitting.

I made it a rule never to say *won't*—as in *I won't drink*—because I believe there's always the possibility that I will. Thinking *won't* is not a good thing for me because I know that if I pick up another drink, I'll never put it down. One drink's too many but a thousand's not enough.

So my strongest attribute is my ability and will to survive, and that's what ultimately makes me a much better person. What doesn't kill you makes you stronger.

A lot of events followed my getting sober that opened my eyes and convinced me that I'd taken the right path. My stepbrother got into a motorcycle accident after doing coke. A week later, he got in a car accident and was killed. Then another guy I partied with died inside a drug shooting gallery. After the third person who worked for me died, I took a long hard look at my great escape. All those guys I'd worked with. Gone. Every one of them died *after* I got sober. I felt as if I'd dodged a bullet.

CHAPTER 6

Paul Jr. at the cemetery at Colville (Omaha Beach), Normandy, France, a World War II shrine. (Photo: Martin GM Kelly)

PAUL JR.: SEED OF A VISION

PAULIE:

The year I was born, 1974, was the year my father bought his first Harley-Davidson. My earliest memory of motorcycles was my father working on his bike, often in pieces or away for paint. He was constantly making changes.

I would ride around town on the back of his bike. That was a big deal. I was young, and it was something we could do together at a time when there wasn't much time together. A lot of his time was spent drinking. My father the alcoholic was the absent father. When he wasn't preoccupied with work and drinking, occasionally we'd go fishing or ride snowmobiles together in the wintertime. It was a big thing to spend any amount of time with my dad. Even when I didn't know that's what I was looking for, I guess I was searching for that "quality time" with my father. When you're a kid and there's dysfunction within the family, somewhere deep inside, you're reaching out for a role model. And a relationship. And acceptance. You want the standard stuff most kids in healthy family relationships simply take for granted or don't appreciate. Those things can play a pretty big part in your life when you have limited time with a parent, like when my father was preoccupied with other things like drinking and hard work.

Although I didn't look at it that way at the time, motorcycles played a significant role in the early stages of my life. During my younger years, I would help my father work on his bike—even if it was just handing him tools—just to be around him when he was tinkering. As a result, I turned very mechanical at an early age. I was interested in moving parts. I was the kid who took things apart. I took *everything* apart because I had to see how things worked. Even if I couldn't put it back together. If it was a game or a toy, I wanted to see what was inside, what made it work. That was me, very curious about the way things operated. I'm like that. A troubleshooter. I like to troubleshoot my way through problems. I like the idea of putting a pile of parts on the table and making something of it, working with what I've got and, if necessary, improvising. I enjoy that. What makes something tick? Why this moving part and what's its function? Why? Why? Why? That's what I love about troubleshooting, using the process of elimination, then narrowing things down by studying the basics of what makes a machine work.

If I'm in front of the TV, I'm watching things most other people won't watch, like documentaries about characters I've never heard of. The how and why of things and certain events in history. How do they mine diamonds? Shows about various species of animals. I see the world as a vast and amazing place. I'll watch a program about the universe, the stars, and the planets. That's what entertains me most: quirky stuff that most people might get bored with or not see the point of. I could watch documentaries around the clock. I love to collect information. I love to know things, as insignificant as they may sometimes seem. I'm that guy who notices what most people don't. Like a spiderweb while going across a bridge at sixty miles an hour. I like picking up on minute details from a distance, close up, or at high speeds.

Nobody taught me design. Once you get the basics of mechanics, you can teach yourself and improve. But design was the thing that was inside me that I didn't know was there while I was growing up. As a kid, I didn't express myself through drawing or painting. I never sculpted in clay. I didn't feel that I had any artistic design talent, particularly at an early age. Once when I was in third grade, we had Fire Prevention Week, where the men from the fire department brought their fire truck down to the school. Our class was assigned a fire prevention project. Since we had a wood-burning stove at my house, and since we would have to clean the chimney constantly, my project dealt with the dangers of chimney fires. I drew a poster on how to prevent them. Of the different fire types—forest fires, house fires, car fires—no one else in the class thought of chimney fires. I won first place, *and* they used my picture. It wasn't the greatest drawing, but the concept worked. And that was the earliest and first time I felt like I could draw or design something that communicated to someone else.

Up until I was about ten years old, I was closest to my mother because my father wasn't around much. My father had to figure things out in his life. Get his priorities straight. So my relationship with my mother was very close. I have a great mother, a phenomenal woman who taught me the value of moral strength. She encouraged us to do the right thing. She urged me to do well in school when my father didn't deal with any of that.

I was terrible in school. I was in special ed classes growing up, and had a hard time with reading comprehension. Throughout school, I had a very short attention span. I was slow at learning. Distracted. Not interested in the classroom. I see a lot of kids today just like me. Maybe we're not real book-smart, but it's not that we're unintelligent, either. Since intelligence can't always be measured by book-smarts, I absolutely hated school. I cried when I had to go. I had an overall fear about the instability of my family situation. Just like my dad, I feared growing up in a broken home. As a result, I was afraid, and I grew up with that fear. Fortunately, I had a gift for design and mechanics that gave me the opportunity to build things.

My mother was an abused wife. Maybe not physically abused, but at least physical bruises go away. It's the mental and emotional abuse that stays with you much longer. I'd much rather take a physical beating and get it over with than to have to deal with the mental scars. It's how we're built as humans. Fortunately, my father made a commitment at some point in his life not to physically abuse us. While he did hit us, and he would lose his temper and we'd get smacked, it wasn't a beating like he got.

Still, the rest of our relationship was bad. There was verbal abuse. The high demands. Things that, when you're a kid, you're not ready to cope with—nor do you know how to cope with. But they affect you nonetheless. The shouting. The impossibly high standards. The rigid and constant work ethic. That kind of abuse was probably more damaging in the long term.

My mother was there for us, but she had severe emotional issues with my father. It was rough for her to be raising three sons (my sister came later) at one time while my father was as bad an alcoholic as they come. For my mother, it was a lot of work just keeping the family together, taking care of the kids, not knowing each night what condition my father would come home in. That was the real suffering. But she was there for us. She did everything to instill values in us. And we were there for each other. The sons were separated by two years apiece, while my sister was four years younger than Michael. As I got older, I became the shoulder my mother could cry on. Although I don't think it was intentional, she would come to me; there might have been no place else for her to go. Being the oldest son of the four children in a dysfunctional alcoholic family, I carried the burden of becoming a man at a very young age.

The turning point in my relationship with my father came when he got sober in 1985. I was about ten when he started taking a keen interest in me, attending all my games. I'd started playing football by the seventh grade. I became a good athlete, and

Paulie (number 44, front row, second from the right)—
one of four team captains of his Valley Central High
School football team. (Photo: OCC Archives)

from the seventh grade until the twelfth, I was a captain of the football team as fullback and linebacker. I played every year—two years in middle school and four years in high school. While the other teams in the Hudson Valley area were way better than us (our school, Valley Central High, was pretty small back then), I was at my best when I competed in sports. Competition ran deep in my family, especially with my father. I became one of the more popular guys at school. I got along with anybody. While the jocks stuck together, I partied and smoked weed and hung out with different kinds of people. I had friends who were rebels and wore Mohawks. I hung out with the kids who came from the city, who were into different kinds of music. Kids with long hair. Jocks. People way smarter than me. The class president. I was a friend with almost everybody. As a result, I was well liked and was not the jerk jock. I was cool with everybody. The teachers liked me. I got into a little trouble now and again, but no real scrapes with the cops or the law. That just wasn't my thing.

One of the first things my father and I did together after he stopped drinking was power lifting and weight lifting. I was twelve when I started power lifting. It was something my father got into, and I was interested as well. In the fourteen- to sixteen-year-old class, I doubled my body weight, not an easy thing to do. I belonged to a power-lifting team. I'd go to a formula meet where they'd take my body weight and subtract it from what I was able to press, along with my age. I held state and national bench press records for kids aged fourteen to sixteen that stood for many years.

While my father and I worked out together, I became one of the strongest kids in *both* middle school and high school. I was benching 275 pounds in the seventh grade, and was the only student in the middle school allowed to work out with the high school kids. I had genetic strength, which came from my grandfather on my mother's side. Paul S. Leonardo was a bear of a man.

Because my father missed out on so many formative years of his sons' lives, once he stopped drinking, the whole issue of him living through me began to rear its head. It was hard for me to deal with. I felt a lot of pressure from him. Yes, he was there for me, but sometimes it was an overbearing and overpowering presence. To this day, I think that his living through me is a big part of our problem working together.

Our relationship is a deep, dark, and complex one, and as a result I'm in touch with a lot of emotions that most people my age probably aren't. I wonder sometimes if, when huge portions of your own family life are blotted out by alcohol, you strongly affect everyone else's life around you once you come back to reality. After those wasted years partying from a pretty early age, my father feels the regrets for those wasted years, like he could have done much more with his family. Now that he has the opportunity to be a bigger part of our lives, while I know he's proud of me, in some ways he's also jealous.

Ten years after my father sobered up, he separated from my mom and left home. I was in my early twenties. It was a lot for a young man to take on. We'd been through years and years of counseling. It was forever a part of my life. I knew about dysfunction, alcoholism, counseling, and fear. For a lot of years, from when I was eight until I was seventeen, we were in counseling, learning from scratch how to be a family once my father quit drinking and rejoined our ranks. Was it hard? It was hard not being the normal family.

Before there were the sports, football games, and power lifting, there was the single most important activity my father and I shared: work. As I got older, I enjoyed working with my hands at my father's Orange County Ironworks business. That was a good thing. Except my father was such a freaking maniac. He was not an easy guy to work for.

Working for my father was a whole different pressure cooker. As a kid, while everyone else had the summer off, I had to work. By the time I was twelve or thirteen, I was already welding, and from that day forward, I worked for my father. While my friends went away on weekends, I stayed behind and worked at the Ironworks Monday through Saturday, for weeks and weeks on end, putting in twelve- and fourteen-hour days. But as a result, I had my own money. I've never been in debt a day in my life. I've never owned a credit card. I was the kid with the cash. I wasn't rich, but I had spending cash. My father and I banged heads over money. He's a very generous person. But when it comes to borrowing money and paying it back, or things of that nature, my father is very strict. There was a quick learning curve regarding the value of money.

When the Teutul sons worked at the Orange County Ironworks, we started at the very bottom. Sweeping up. Painting and dipping rails into huge paint tanks. I went through every stage of development inside the Ironworks. Fortunately, I could weld right off the bat. I picked up on that quickly. Then I was promoted to running the railing department, which was a large portion of OCI's business. I ran railings for a few years, creating my own system of doing things adapted from, yet different from, what the older guys who had been in the shop for years had developed. And when I say *ran* a department, bear in mind that in my father's shop there was no such thing as a supervisor. We had forty employees, and we worked under the title of "working foremen." That meant that when I was the foreman of the railing department, I *worked;* I never just supervised. Throughout the years, the steel business would go up and down in terms of workloads. We had our good years, and we had our slow times. But I was expected to, and did, stay busy.

My father expected a lot more from me than from anyone else who worked for him. As his oldest son, I was, and still am, held to the highest standard. Regarding the business, my father saw only two possible extremes. One was starting a family business where the father is very lenient and lets the kids do whatever they want until he retires, hands them the reins, then watches them run it into the ground. Or second: He expects more from his sons than from the rest of the workers, while expectations for the rest of the workers were very high to begin with. Which of these became our working model? Guess.

Just before we formed Orange County Choppers, working with my father at the Ironworks was extremely tough. There was little or no separation between work and family life. It got so twisted and intertwined as resentment built up; it started at work and then followed us at home, and unfortunately it didn't stop. Yet my father has always wanted me around. It's like he had to have me around. It's just a thing with him. If he has somewhere to go, he wants to make sure I'm going to be there with him. In some ways, it's out of love. Does he love me? Yes. And I love him.

My father definitely has an obsession with hard work, and the term *workaholic* doesn't begin to describe him. I'll give you a perfect example of his craziness. When I was eighteen, living at home and working at the Ironworks, we had a huge snowstorm. Our driveway dipped down and we had eight feet of enormous snowdrifts. And we were going to work! The roads were shut down, and we were going to work! Nobody was going to be around when we got there because it was a state of emergency. Still, my father started up the pickup and was trying to get out of the driveway like a crazy, obsessed maniac. As we tried to back out, we got hopelessly stuck in eight feet of snow, stranded in the middle of the driveway. That's the madness I dealt with.

Stable, my father is not. But what he has is drive. What areas he might be lacking—in business sense or education—he makes up for in sheer determination. He has that unstoppable drive to succeed that most people will never achieve. He's always been driven to succeed, and that's what's made him successful. I may not agree with what he does, but his drive is something you can't argue with.

My mother instilled my personal values, as far as maintaining a strong and grounded moral standing, which came from a Christian upbringing and being a Christian. Then as we got older, we made decisions on our own. So I didn't always walk the straight and narrow. God knows I was far from perfect. I went into rehab when I was sixteen. I was young, I know, and I don't know if I had such an extreme problem, but at least I got straight. A group of my friends went into rehab at different times. There were six or seven of us guys at age sixteen, going to drug rehab meetings and counseling together. And while my friends were into different things that were a little heavier, I was a bad pothead. I was stoned all the time, every day. Stoned became normal. For years, and after rehab for a time, I'd occasionally drift back out there and start partying again. It became a vicious cycle that went on and on. Then I found that pot sucked the inspiration out of me, and I squashed it. I overcame it.

I believe as individuals, how we are brought up, and how our personalities are formed, we may be a lot like our fathers. But we are not our fathers. I am not my father. My youngest brother, Michael, is a big teddy bear. He was one of the biggest kids in his class and somewhat athletic. But he couldn't play football because he just didn't have it in him to hit people. It was just not in his disposition. As for me, if that's what the situation calls for on the field, I can hit people. I'll stand up for myself. My father doesn't scare me like he intimidates other people. That's why I stand up to him. I bark back. I've dealt with him my whole life. So yes, I'll stand up to him, and I'll fight when I have to.

As for our success with Orange County Choppers, I've had a premonition about it. It stemmed from coming from a Christian home, knowing right from wrong, and feeling like God had a plan. I've always felt and known something big was going to happen to us, even before the bikes or the TV show came along. I didn't know quite what it would be, but I wasn't surprised when it happened. People ask me, Can you believe what's happened to your family in the past few years? I say no. We can't believe the fame and fortune, but somehow I knew that life was going to be great.

Like a divine gift, back when we first started building bikes, before we took off as builders, I knew something great was going to come out of this. Something wonderful, something blow-me-away fantastic. Although I had no interest in television or fame, I just knew we would be well known in front of large groups of people. Don't ask me how or why or what I knew.

I just knew.

I had a premonition, the seed of a vision.

The True Blue Bike was one of the first to roll out of the basement as part of the Basement Bike collection. A classic Pro Street model, it was one of Senior and Paulie's earliest collaborations. (Photo: OCC Archives)

TRUE BLUE AND THE HOT ROD CHOPPER

PAULIE:

Before there was such a thing as an Orange County Chopper, we loved the idea of customizing bikes on our own. My father busted his hump on the Sunshine Bike, which was the final incarnation of his 1974 Harley-Davidson Superglide. He had transformed his main ride from a drab AMF-era Harley road hog to a sparkling, cherried-out, cherry-red customized Old School two-wheeler with extended chrome pipes, handsome flame work on the tank (featuring a smiling sun) and back fender, and shiny retro spoke wheels.

By 1985, my father and mother had split up and gone their separate ways. Dad found himself living the single life in a rented apartment in Montgomery on the corner of Beaver Dam and Goodwill Roads. Throughout the late 1980s and into the '90s, he had successfully remained sober. No more drunken craziness; no more boozing and getting loaded. He was alcohol- and drug-free, but he was still a compulsive maniac. His drinking days were behind him, and so were the days of endless family counseling sessions and 12-step program meetings.

By 1995, my father was in the mood to reinvent himself. He thought about putting his workaholic days at the Ironworks shop behind him. He wanted to get away from the long hours and endless demands of the steel business. He had toiled his life away, twelve to fourteen hours a day at a time, absent from his family. And to what end? He was stuck in a rented apartment. He damn near killed himself with alcohol and drugs. Now he wanted to just be an unattached guy, and for the first time in his life, he pictured himself semi-retired. He had a few bucks stashed away for retirement. At the time—along with Danny and Mikey—I was working at Orange County Ironworks, heading up the railings department, which was the busiest department of the shop.

It was the perfect time for my father to start thinking about entering a new phase of his life. At this point, bikes were more important to him than anything—specifically, custom cycles. He could take apart a rigid-frame Harley with his eyes closed. He restored a 1977 Harley FL and chopped it. His specialty was working rigid and swing-arm frames and chopping them into stretched-out road hogs. In my opinion, he was stuck in a style that was deeply rooted in the 1960s and '70s, banging out a sweetened-up, customized FLH Full Dresser. He would change the wheels and add big ape hanger handlebars. He dug ape hangers, and loved to turn his friends on to them. He said that once you get used to them, it was the most comfortable way to ride. My father was Old School all the way in his early basement days. That was his only style. It was what he knew. Everything else to him was junk. Softails and EVOs were the enemy. There was nothing you could say to convince him otherwise.

Pretty soon, he started spending more of his time away from the shop. My father spent endless hours tinkering on motorcycles and lifting weights down in the basement. Being the overachieving, compulsive fanatic that he is, my father would get up and go into his basement at seven o'clock in the morning and stay down there until after ten at night. He didn't have to answer the phone if he didn't want to. He had his own little paradise, and he knew where everything was and had his tools spread out just right. There was nobody around to mess with him and piss him off.

It was a genuine hobby for him. I was working away nine to five in the steel shop, but pretty soon, as is the case with my father, his hobby would become an obsession. He dreamed of building bikes for a living, with the goal of having them laid out in sexy glossy bike magazines like *Playboy* centerfolds. My father looked up to those chopper and Harley magazines. *Iron Horse* and *Easyriders*. Mikey loved to sift through the pile and find the ones with the nude girls sitting on top of the bikes. The basement days were an interesting time for my father. For the first time in his life, he could be left alone to drink coffee all day, wrench up bikes, and ponder his next move in relative solitude.

My father was primarily an individual rider. A loner on the open road.

Growing up, we didn't have loads of guys horsing around the front yard on motorcycles or doing wheelies up and down the block. He'd have a few guys he would putt around with once in a while, but not large packs or anything. Besides, the small town of Montgomery wasn't necessarily amenable to large groups of bike riders. He freaked out the townspeople enough during his inebriated days at the steel shop in the center of the village.

As I mentioned, my dad bought his first Harley the year I was born. From then on, he has always worked on it. One of my earliest memories of motorcycles is the first time my father took his '74 Superglide apart. He did a full restoration on it, and he had the whole bike completely torn apart downstairs in the basement. He labeled each piece meticulously. We had a table set up with the parts beautifully spread out. At the time, the family had a crazy Great Dane, and by mistake my father once left him downstairs. Thanks to the dog, when he came home, the whole basement was covered with errant motorcycle parts. I remember we had to put them in a barrel and figure it out from there. It was like assembling a *basket case*—a motorcycle term for a Harley, in pieces, in a box. That was an education in itself.

When it wasn't riding season, the Sunshine Bike was apart and away for paint. He made constant changes on that one bike. Looking back, I think my father wanted to get me interested in motorcycles so we could work together on them, just like when he took a rabid interest in Danny and me playing high school sports, or when the two of us formed our own power-lifting team. I feel like my dad has had this strange dependence on getting me involved with any new project he wanted to attempt.

While my father's first bike was a Triumph, in 1995 he built me a bike out of a custom frame and an EVO motor he picked out especially for me. That project marked the first bike the two of us seriously collaborated on. It was an important bike in the history of OCC in that it had a definite chopper slant to it, although the appeal of choppers had long since faded by the mid-1990s.

But the two of us always admired choppers. Way before I was into designing bikes, if I had a choice, I preferred the look and curvature of choppers to the standard assembly-line bikes built by Harley-Davidson. Of course, my father worshipped choppers back in the 1970s after watching the *Easy Rider* movie and during his hell-on-wheels crazy days. Aesthetically, not knowing a ton about them when I first started designing bikes with my dad, I liked the look of a chopper over regular bikes. It was much, much cooler.

Anyway, the first serious customizing job we did together was when my father and I built the bike from the ground up. We painted the frame black, and, just like the

Sunshine Bike, it had yellow hot rod flames on it. A guy named George at RSM Custom Paint painted the bike and the flames for us. George was local; he lived up in the mountains in a place called Pine Bush. He was an old hot rod painter from Long Island who also painted '70s Triumph bikes, which is how my father knew about him.

When we modified my bike, unlike nowadays, we collaborated on the design. Its retro Old School look was a style my dad was very familiar with. We worked together getting it going. On that particular bike, he gave me ideas and I went ahead and did a lot of the fabrication.

Fabrication is the act of making something out of steel; the shaping and forming of bars and sheets of steel. Sheet metal, for instance, comes in round form or flat. If it's flat, you can pound out gas tanks. If it's round, you can bend it. It's that simple.

Fabrication is an extensive process, which I had no trouble with since I had so much experience welding at the Ironworks. I fabricated the oil tank, and I learned how to cut half tanks and weld them together to give them that extended, flowing look. My father and I both worked on fabricating a new chain guard and belt guard. We ran a chain and sprocket instead of a belt and pulley. We made it look like an Old School chopper with a modern engine.

We called it "Paulie's Black with Yellow Flames Bike." My father knew about modifying Harleys or building from scratch, except this one turned into much more of a chopper than the Sunshine Bike did. Actually, after we customized it, we named it the Hot Rod Chopper. Looking back, it was a pretty radical bike for its time, the 1990s, because we raked and stretched the frame ourselves. If you look closely at the Hot Rod Chopper, you'll see that pull-and-dip-out contour of the handlebars, which is where our whole current style of standard handlebars evolved. Those were my idea, and I built them myself. We installed the speedometer into its own shroud where the handlebars went into the frame. We put a late-style Arlen Ness front end on it with a flat fender on the rear.

The Hot Rod Chopper is a classic early OCC design. It had an old-style frame with a new motor. Actually, when I think about it, we mostly worked on that bike in the Ironworks shop. We built that black bike just before we started building bikes together in my father's basement. To this day, my father is proud of that bike. I'm surprised at how ahead of its time the Hot Rod Chopper was. It was a nice-looking bike. We made it work. When we finished that bike, creating a company was something we thought about a little, but we weren't too sure we were going to do it. After we started the company later on, we sold the bike to keep ourselves afloat. And my father still gripes about it.

ORANGE COUNTY CHOPPERS

Paulie's Black with Yellow Flames Bike, later renamed the Hot Rod Chopper, was originally photographed to appear in a bike magazine, but the negatives were lost in the shuffle. (Photo: OCC Archives)

"That bike was a nice freaking bike," he likes to remind me. "I can kick myself in the balls all day long for getting rid of that one."

The important thing to remember about that time when we first started building bikes together—and before we officially formed Orange County Choppers—was that choppers were not popular. They had faded away after the 1970s. It wasn't until Jesse James's West Coast Choppers designs helped popularize the look of late-1960s/early-1970s choppers again that they came back in style.

By the late 1990s, the hot look in customized motorcycles was called the Pro Street look. Just before we started building our bikes, the Pro Street look was heading toward the end of its ten-to-fifteen-year reign. Most customized bikes in the magazines and at the custom car and bike shows were Pro Streets. By definition, Pro Street bikes are low and long. Not up and stretched up, but raked out and lower to the ground. They usually featured a rounded tank with a fairly large capacity, but the whole look was decidedly low and clean. That's what was hot in 1997.

After we built the Hot Rod Chopper, our next bikes were definitely more influenced by the Pro Street look. Add a little stretch, sneak in a little rake. Make it lower and longer, but not as exaggerated as a chopper. Then after that, when Jesse started building outright choppers, that renewed interest in choppers; they became the next big thing. Although we had done the Hot Rod Chopper much earlier, by around 2000 we started building full-blown choppers.

Although my father and I have fought and argued a lot in the steel shop, he's managed to reach out and get me involved with almost everything he's worked on. It was no different when he started building bikes in his basement. As often as he's pissed off with me, I was a phone call away when he needed me. When I was running the railing shop and he had semi-retired, he would call and ask for my help with some spot welding. From the very first bike he had built, I helped him fabricate it. Compared with the bikes today, there wasn't a lot of fabrication to do, except the fenders and gas tanks. But that kinda started us off working together. I would come down and give him a hand in the middle of the day, when I was supposed to be back at OCI making sure the rails were getting done. My father kept pulling me away from the shop when he needed help. I was a crack welder, and after the Hot Rod Chopper, I became more and more interested in designing my own bikes, too. But since I was younger, I leaned toward the more modern Pro Street look, rather than the Old School retro designs my dad liked.

I remember when my dad was first inspired—challenged, actually—to build his first Pro Street bike. In 1997, he had ridden down to Daytona for Biketoberfest with a bunch of guys, most of whom were a lot younger than he was. They had hot companies around the bike show, like Big Dog and Titan, showing off their aftermarket customized bikes that were getting really popular. A couple of the guys he rode with ended up buying these bikes. They forked out a potful of money for these machines, and my father told them matter-of-factly, "Man, I can build those bikes for half that price."

His friends didn't buy his rap for a minute.

"Aww, screw you," they told him. "You can build them old tinkers, but you ain't building nothing like this."

Softails first came out in 1985. The Harley-Davidson Softail frame is designed to resemble the more traditional rigid bikes of the past, while offering a more comfortable ride complete with rear suspension. Shock absorbers are situated along the axis of the motorcycle, tucked away under the transmission. My father never messed with those kinds of bikes. They were the enemy bikes. He dealt only with motorcycles made in 1984 and earlier. He knew rigids and swing arms inside and out, and stubbornly stayed away from any modern styles.

The second new Harley-Davidson my father bought was a 1985 FXWG, which he also owns today. It was the last of the square-style swing arms with a four-speed kick-start and an eighty-inch EVO motor, which was Harley's most dependable engine at the time. It was an odd-year Harley model because that was the year they went with the Softails, so they made only a certain number of this FXWG style of frame.

But down at Daytona, my dad wanted to prove those younger guys wrong. True, he was more into the older rigid-frame stuff. His whole concept of motorcycles was stuck in the dark ages. Every time he looked inside a biker magazine, he'd go straight for the older Harleys and flip past the hot new Softail bikes that other builders were raving about. Softails were the enemy for him back then, but they were the most happening Harley style at the time. He saw customized Softails selling for about thirty-five thousand bucks, which, at the time, was top dollar, a lot of money.

As soon as he came home from Daytona, he went back down to his basement workshop. At first he was pretty low-key about it. He didn't tell anybody that he was designing and working on a Pro Street bike from scratch. He ordered himself a Softail frame. Then, when he got the frame delivered, he picked up a ton of Arlen Ness parts. He started working on the bike, and when he had most of it built, he called me in to add some custom fabrication. I was intrigued, and this time I had some design ideas of my own to add to the mix. I mounted the rear fender to the swing arm using internal struts. We figured the coolest thing to do was to get rid of the struts and put them inside the fenders to make it look seamless and clean. Most Softails had struts on the outside, which, to me, breaks up the lines. Back then, you didn't see a lot of that. My fender seemed to float over the tire. It wasn't a major thing; I just cut this fender to a point and welded the mounts on the frame for the tank. I helped my dad put the motor in, and we assembled the front end. We finished the bike together. Like the theme bikes we would build later, my father liked to name the bikes when they were finished. He called this one True Blue because of the pearl tone of royal blue we had chosen.

The True Blue Bike was the first official OCC project to roll out of the basement. Instead of restoring a bike, we built this one from scratch, and it felt good. True Blue started the next generation of what we were doing. True Blue was the first Pro Street we had worked on. My father told me that in coming up with the look, a Jim Nasi bike he had seen in a magazine inspired him.

When we brought that bike out of the basement and people saw that it was a modern Pro Street Softail, everybody agreed that it was awesome. When we showed the bike to our friends, they freaked out. My father had never had anything to do with these kinds of bikes before. He hated them. But he had proven his buddies wrong. We knew we had something right away, as the reactions spoke pretty strongly. But it was a risk, like anything else.

The whole experience with True Blue piqued my interest because once the bike was done and we painted it that nice rich blue color, this thing was like a spaceship! "Now you got my attention!" I told my dad. "This is cool stuff we can do together."

My father had joined the 1990s, and once we built that first Softail, he took a gradual liking to more and more contemporary custom bikes. He was straying from his safe world of Panhead, Knucklehead, and Shovelhead motors, and going over to the enemy, the EVO motor.

Everywhere we went with that bike, we snapped necks. In essence, it was a glorified Harley Softail, yet it was pretty functional with its big half tanks. Since my dad was in charge of ordering the parts, we used a lot of Arlen Ness stuff. We didn't have any wholesale connections, so in the early going we had to pay full-whack retail for the parts. Later on, we were able to get a dealer price on parts when we began buying enough stuff off folks like Arlen Ness and Custom Chrome. Otherwise, for these early bikes, we paid retail.

After we finished True Blue, my father made up his mind. He would spend whatever it took, and we would build six or seven more bikes and sell them at bike shows. Always the first guy to leap off the bridge, he was prepared to spend a ton of his own money on building more bikes. He had money stashed away for retirement, but for him, the risk-taker, retirement was now a gamble on half a dozen custom bikes. He was on a roll. So we built our first six or seven bikes completely out of pocket, with no special orders, no nothing. It was complete insanity. My father took a huge risk with his own money, his future.

Looking back, if we hadn't gotten the television show off the ground, it could have been a disaster that wiped my father out financially. Nobody knew we were going to become a phenomenon, but that was the risk he took, and thank God it worked out.

On that note, I say, hats off to my father. He went for it, took the blind leap, and didn't think twice.

The Silver Bike, another Basement Bike creation. Note the opulent paint job and destined-to-be-classic OCC design. (Photo: OCC Archives)

MORE BRAWN THAN BRAINS: PRO STREETS AND BASEMENT BIKES

PAULIE:

After we finished True Blue, my father and I didn't rest on our laurels . . . or our hardies. My father put his money where his mouth was and yanked out $120,000 from his savings and retirement accounts. I was dividing my time between the steel shop and working with my father in his basement designing bikes. During the rainy season, water would leak in and our basement work space would flood. We'd be slogging around in a few inches of water, watching parts boxes float around while we worked. It's a wonder we didn't get electrocuted. We were in enough potential hot water as it was, being holed up in a residential apartment complex not zoned for industrial work. Mainly, we did the fabrication at the Ironworks, but the assembly process was mostly done in my father's basement.

The Yellow Bike was the second chopper we made after the Hot Rod Chopper. It was our third customized project overall, and it was ahead of its time, too. As with True Blue, my father had an idea of how he wanted to build the bike, but the more fabrication we used, the more involved I got in the design.

The Yellow Bike had more extensive fabrication done on it than the Sunshine Bike, True Blue, and Hot Rod Chopper. We stretched the tubes. We fabricated the exhaust and different kinds of brackets; we made our own belt drive cover, chain guard, and license plate bracket. We took just stock half tanks. We used highly chromed spoke wheels with a size 200 back tire. The coup de grâce was when we added a Frank Frazetta–type paint design on the gas tank. On one side was a warrior hulk mushing across the snow with a team of polar bears. Frazetta did a lot of Dungeons and Dragons artwork and album covers for the southern rock band Molly Hatchet. My father picked out the image and had a painter copy the artwork.

The Yellow Bike exhibits early Teutul flash. It's the third bike Paulie and Senior built together. (Photo: OCC Archives)

Of all of our initial bikes, that was the one that stood out. No matter where we traveled with that motorcycle—to bike and car shows or poker runs—people gathered around it. It displayed the early Teutul flash. We had this certain indescribable flair, and each bike had a personal touch that reached out to people.

My father loved studying bikes. The lines, the flow, the different models. A lot of his early inspiration came from the motorcycle magazines. *Street Chopper. Easyriders.* He collected all the issues starting in the 1960s and had three stacks of magazines six feet high. Every time he wanted to build a bike, he'd start at the top and go through all three stacks, just to get ideas. Then he would take pieces of different bikes—this fender, that motor, those foot pegs, these handlebars—and that's how he'd flesh out his ideas. His first Ironworks partner, Fred Gerini, was also his first major influence.

We spent about thirty thousand dollars building the Yellow and True Blue Bikes. And we weren't done yet. We wanted to build an awesome lineup of bikes and put them out on the road. We wanted each bike to have a continuing theme, similar to True Blue—like when a fashion designer shows off a new spring or fall line of clothing. They would be built in the Pro Street style, not choppers, with top-grade Arlen Ness accessories. As we did with True Blue, we picked some primo colors right off a color chart and went to work.

Just like when Bob Dylan recorded *The Basement Tapes,* these became "the Basement Bikes." They were the earliest OCC creations, made even before we officially formed the company. We were either nuts or naive. It didn't matter to us that we had no financial backers or customers lined up beforehand. We didn't care that there were hundreds of bike builders across the country that had been doing this for decades. We just believed in ourselves. We figured we would blow everybody away and sell out our complete line.

For the Basement Bikes, we decided to use rich, luxuriant tones and keep them sleek, simple, and classy. There were six Basement Bikes, built in 1998 and 1999. They were done in very basic hues and were constructed in this order: (1) Blue, (2) Yellow, (3) Silver, (4) Orange, (5) Candy-Apple Green with orange flames and yellow pinstripe, and (6) classic Red.

The Silver Bike was gorgeous and served as a sequel to True Blue. We used the Blue Bike as the basis for getting into a modern one-two-punch type of production feel, flow, and continuity. Elegant. Silky. The actual color was Snow White Pearl, and it looked opulent. The Silver Bike was designed in tandem with True Blue. The rear fender came to a little different point, and we used a similar larger tank. The two bikes looked breathtaking going down the road together side by side. Very basic, but entirely sophisticated.

After the Silver Bike, we built the Orange Bike. I was getting more involved by this time. The headlights on the Basement Bikes looked futuristic. We closed the neck down a little more. I took Harley half tanks again, spliced them together, and then cut an arc on the bottom. The Orange Bike was cool because you could see the subtle design curve among them. They were modern Pro Streets with a good stretch

ORANGE COUNTY CHOPPERS

The Orange Bike was one of the six Basement Bikes originally financed from Senior's retirement nest egg, before there was such a thing as Orange County Choppers. (Photo: OCC Archives)

in the backbone, but nothing sweeping upward; it was stretched out, low and long, and not an ominous chopper style.

Like the yellow Frazetta cycle, the Green Bike with its orange flames was another eye-catcher with a little more splash-and-flash paint. We used a candy-apple green with an orange flame accented with a yellow pinstripe. It had a bigger 230-size rear tire, which was not a functional tire for that style of bike, but it looked supercool. The Green Bike was our first fat-tire bike. As with the Yellow Bike, we used Old School spoke wheels. Then I took the fender from the basement to the shop, cut a crazy pattern out of it, trimmed it with round bar, and put in some mesh. I did the front fender in the same manner. We cut it a little short in the front and let it flip down so it matched. It was a cool bike.

ORANGE COUNTY CHOPPERS

The Green Bike, with its pointed back fender and orange flame job, features the distinct Paul Jr. fabrication style that would appear in subsequent OCC chopper designs. (Photo: OCC Archives)

The Red Bike was candy-apple red and built close to the ground. Except for the modern wheels, the Red Bike looked more retro than the others. This was the Old School bike of the collection, complete with a Harley Panhead motor. I designed the exhaust system to come up through the other side. The two candy-apple-colored bikes, the Red and Green, complemented each other.

Through the process of building, customizing, and modifying seven bikes together, the working relationship between my father and me shaped and defined itself. I was the main fabricator, my father would oversee the assembly process, and the two of us would collaborate on designs. But as we evolved into creating more New School bike designs and fewer Old School and retro ideas, I took an increased interest in most of the design aspects of our bikes. My father relied on me to come up with the newest design innovations that would put us ahead of the pack.

The Red Bike, powered by a Harley-Davidson Knucklehead, reflects the OCC retro Old School flash that would find its way into Senior's later builds. (Photo: OCC Archives)

Like I said, I had no training in mechanical drawing. I didn't take any art classes in school, nor was there any time for me to attend a design college. I had no computer graphics training, and I couldn't draw very well. Although I didn't have a lot of book training, I was becoming a good fabricator. In seeing my designs come to life, I adopted a more seat-of-the-pants approach.

I decided to build bikes straight out of my head.

In the days of the Basement Bikes, our main design innovations sprang from my head. Like I did when I took over the railing department, I invented my own methods of development. I rarely drew anything out with superprecise blueprint-style measurements. Fifty percent of the bike was planned: I could visualize how I wanted to do it in my head before I started. Then the other 50 percent would come along as the bike started to take on form. Today I do it a little bit that way, but nowadays we have more fabricators and designers involved, so it's easier to give the larger group a preliminary visual picture and let everyone do their part. In the early days, though, it was *Measure once and fire up the torch.*

Many artists will tell you that the most exciting part of doing creative things like building bikes, making TV shows, acting in movies, or writing books isn't the finished work per se; it's the ongoing process, complete with the trial and error of experimentation. God knows, a lot of screwups, miscalculations, and last-minute additions and deletions go on in the shop with most of our bikes.

Three stages of the bike building process are my favorites. The first is when ideas are coming from my head to my hands, and I'm bringing concepts to life. The second is when I'm completely done fabricating the parts. There's a certain reward, the feeling of a milestone, in getting to that juncture. The third stage I particularly enjoy is putting the bike together after everything arrives back at the shop completely chromed, painted, and powder-coated (a baked color-coating process used for the frame and other main parts).

Looking back at the Basement Bikes, I think we experimented more with custom fabrication than most other builders at that time, mostly because my dad and I both came from such a broad, hands-on background in steel fabrication, as well as having the right heavy equipment to do it. While most builders were pounding out tanks, sending out their fabricating, and bolting on aftermarket accessories and parts, we started cutting our own fenders, welding round bar, and doing different things with a unique custom flair. That would later manifest itself with a custom cycle called the Spider Man Bike, our very first theme bike, where we used special webbing around the tank and the sissy bar. Not too many people were fabricating intricate detailed stuff like that, but we'll get to the Spider Man Bike phenomenon later on.

My father had pretty much left the main fabrication duties to me after we first started working together. Although he was a great fabricator in his time, he lost the drive or the will to keep doing it. Back when he ran the Ironworks with his partners, he did a tremendous amount of fabrication and set up the heavy machinery in the shop. He would build jigs and do multiple kinds of punch work on large structural steel projects like stairwells and railings. He was a master at it, but there came a point when he stopped enjoying it because of the pressure.

For me, fabricating bikes and fabricating stuff like railings were two different animals. To set up a steel shop and do structural steel and other industrial work involved a whole different left-brain/right-brain mechanical aspect than building Pro

Streets, bobbers, and choppers. Once I moved my skills into the direction of motorcycle design, I entered a whole new world where I had to rely more on my own creativity. As I did that, I became more my own person, and less my father's son. I think my father realized that I had a better eye for design and a more modern vision working with Softails and newer bikes, as opposed to his style of retro modification. Old School bike building was simple because it was so raw and basic, but in my opinion—and I know my father would emphatically disagree—you're not creating something as magical.

While my father loves modern bikes, he has an undying passion for older-style bikes. I just don't have the historical perspective that he does. I appreciate them and I think they're great. I admire some builders like the late Indian Larry, and I love to study their bikes as works of art. I think they're neat, but unlike me, my father has a personal history riding those bikes. I don't. I wasn't a die-hard bike rider when I was a young guy. It's not a part of my rugged and wild past like it was for him.

When you get right down to it, I am a New School bike designer and my father is rooted in the Old. My past started with the new bikes after 1985, especially when my dad and I built the Basement Bikes together. I love the old influences. I love the integration of styles, and we have discussions (and arguments) about this constantly. I appreciate all kinds of traditional design, even outside motorcycles, but my father is sometimes overly passionate about the Old School bikes. While to me they're cool—and obviously, most motorcycle design patterns are based on the basic lines and flow—I prefer the modern look with an occasional, unmistakable Old School twist. I think that with us coming onto the scene at the tail end of the Pro Street era, the Basement Bikes had an attention-grabbing combination of the traditional and the contemporary.

After the summer of 1999, the time came to pursue the business by leaving the basement of my father's house and moving into a bike shop of our own. We didn't have to look very far. The most logical thing to do was to move our little enterprise directly into the Orange County Ironworks building. By this time, my brother Danny had taken over the steel shop, and I was spending most of my time designing bikes.

We made room for the bike shop down in the basement in a fifty-by-fifty-foot area. We had to figure out a name for the business when we filled out the paperwork to start the company. My father plainly stated that we would call our new bike business Orange County Choppers. It was typical of my dad to keep things simple, and he already had Orange County Ironworks.

Orange County Choppers. It didn't sound very flashy to me; it wasn't a very sexy name for a chopper and motorcycle company. But we didn't have a bunch of alternative choices, so I reluctantly agreed and decided we'd make it work. I sat down at the kitchen table at my mom's house one night after work and developed a logo.

Sometimes a logo can make or break your company. It's on your letterhead, on T-shirts, in advertising, publicity, banners, and flyers. Corporations hire roomfuls of experts to do them. I hadn't done anything like that before. All I had was this name, Orange County Choppers, and I was thinking it was not, well, the most exciting name. But that's what I had to work with. It ended up to be a blessing in disguise, though, having the initials *OCC*. I used those letters to make a sleek chopper logo. If it had been any other name, it wouldn't have worked out and assumed the shape of a chopper. The logo contoured like an actual bike, because *it is* a bike. I drew just one design and put it away. Then I brought it in to work the next day and drew the new logo on the shop floor. We still have the original piece of paper. That logo, although it's a little bit more elongated and stretched out, is the same one we use today.

CHAPTER

The Basement Bikes on retail display for the first time at the Auto Toy Store in Fort Lauderdale. (Photo: OCC Archives)

ONWARD TO DAYTONA

SENIOR:

After we finished the Basement Bikes, we had our own shop site and a traveling stable of hot customized motorcycles. It was time to hit the road and display our wares. We were anxious to debut our new collection at the 1999 Biketoberfest in Daytona Beach. We brought down our entire line of Basement Bikes, plus the Hot Rod Chopper and a few others.

It was a bitch riding down from New York to Florida. I picked up a motor home that was pretty funky inside and was hard to keep on the highway. Behind it we towed a large cumbersome trailer where we kept the bikes. It was an eleven-hundred-mile journey down the East Coast to Florida, and ordinarily it took about twenty hours. But for us, it took three days to make that day-and-a-half trip because our tires would keep blowing out at night. Then we would have to wait until the next day to change them or get a new set of wheels. The trailer would be swaying back and forth across the road like a drunk driver. It seemed as if we were getting pulled over by the cops every time we crossed another state line.

In the beginning, when we rolled into Daytona, we felt like everybody else was way more organized than us rookie bike builders. When we opened the back of the trailer, we were shocked to see how badly the load had shifted. Our bikes were lying all over the place, strewn on their sides with lawn chairs and spare tires spread out on top of them. The other established bike builders like Paul Yaffe, Eddie Trotta, Arlen Ness, all those guys I read about in bike magazines, would drive into Daytona in their semis with a full staff or road crew. The top guys had air-conditioned portable showrooms with plush leather couches to sit on inside special trailers displaying their latest bikes. In contrast, Paulie and I were stuck outside with the hot Florida sun beating down on us, sitting in old lawn chairs with six bikes parked out in front of us. We didn't even have business cards.

Once we had our spot picked out and our bikes lined up for display, it was time for the big sell. We'd do anything it took to grab attention, establish ourselves, and make our new venture work. Before we left New York, we had spent a ton of money to hire a photographer to take professional pictures of our bikes, in case we needed to show them to any magazine editors or potential clients. Although there were nearly half a million motorcycle enthusiasts at Biketoberfest, it was a dogfight just to get anybody's attention. Everybody and their brother who had a decent ride came to Daytona and wanted the motorcycle magazines to notice them and run pictures of their bikes to legitimize themselves as bike builders and help develop a clientele.

An editor named Howard from *Hot Bike* ("the Harley-Davidson enthusiast's magazine") was walking through Biketoberfest and came across us. At the time, this was the number one magazine on the newsstands, and the guy had his eye on Paulie's Hot Rod Chopper and a red Panhead chopper that had a cool coffin-shaped gas tank Paulie had built from scratch. Then the editor took a long look at the Green Bike with the orange flame job. Howard from *Hot Bike* left and came back later with his photo team. They freaked out at our collection of bikes, made by Orange County Choppers, this Hudson Valley father-and-son team that nobody had heard of. They didn't want to let on, but they were excited with our concepts. The *Hot Bike* people told us they wanted to shoot our bikes and put them in their magazine.

We set up three sessions for *Hot Bike* to photograph the Green Bike, the red Panhead with the coffin-shaped tank, and my Hot Rod Chopper on location in Daytona. The Green Bike and the Panhead later appeared in *Hot Bike* in their own photo spreads about two months apart, in March and May 2001. Funny enough, the magazine lost the negatives for the original Hot Rod Chopper session. We would *love* to find those lying around somewhere.

It was the very first time our work had appeared in a national magazine. I was pleased and proud. I had achieved one of my early objectives as a fledgling bike builder. Our next goal was to sell the bikes we'd forked out our hard-earned cash for and make some money.

Near the end of Daytona, another group of guys we didn't know came by and said they loved our bikes. "Why don't you bring these bikes down to the Auto Toy Store?" they suggested. This was an exotic car shop in Fort Lauderdale that catered to a super-rich customer base. They had everything from Bentleys to Enzo Ferraris lined up in a giant showroom. At first we thought they were BS'ing us. Then they said they would call us tomorrow, and sure enough, some rich blue blood from the Auto Toy Store phoned the next day from his helicopter. We loaded up the trailer, started up the motor home, and headed for Fort Lauderdale. We wound up putting our bikes on their showroom floor. They looked spectacular alongside the luxury Italian sports cars. We were pumped up.

Between the Auto Toy Store and Biketoberfest, we were gone for about a month. I had brought my girlfriend at the time and my dog down with us, and we lived in the motor home and took in the warm Florida breeze.

The long and the short of it was that we thought we'd hit this big home run, us being around the rich and famous customers at the Auto Toy Store. But nothing monetary came out of it. We had a good time, and it was great fun for the billionaire playboy types who came by to check out our stuff. But in our whole monthlong trip to Florida, we didn't sell a single bike. Still, seeing our bikes lined up next to a fleet of Ferraris made us believe more that our bikes were going to be a hot commodity someday.

In the final analysis, we were satisfied with the reactions our bikes got at that first Daytona show. It inspired us to go on. We had shocked people, and the magazine companies loved us right off the bat because we had something different. We vowed to keep coming out with new cool bikes.

Back in the 1990s, you had to be in love with custom bikes to buy them. The registration and title process was a bitch. As a result of Daytona, we scored a lead to go on to Myrtle Beach, South Carolina, to visit a guy who owned a Ford car dealership. To our amazement, he bought five of our bikes in one shot. That was a huge help in the money department, and since he was a car dealer, he had ways to figure out how to get them registered for insurance and license.

A year later, we hit another streak of good luck and found a way to get our bikes registered and titled. Since we weren't licensed manufacturers of our bikes in New York State at that time, it proved to be a real hassle to register any of our machines and make them street-worthy. If somebody bought one of our bikes at that time, they'd

A page from OCC's very first professional sales brochure featured the earliest company logos as well as a collection of the Basement Bikes. (Photo: OCC Archives)

have to go through weeks or months of registration. For instance, if we wanted to register our Basement Bikes in New York, we needed to send all kinds of photo documentation up to Albany. If the folks there didn't like what we sent them, then we would have to make the necessary changes and alterations. It all took ages, and

A page torn out of motorcycle history: OCC's first paid full-page ad appeared in **Street Chopper** *magazine, spring 2002. (Photo: OCC Archives)*

afterward, you might just end up with a junk title or a kit title. It wouldn't bear the name of a licensed manufacturer. To make matters worse, New York's insurance restrictions were a headache for aftermarket bikes, too. A lot of insurance companies would say, "If you're not a manufacturer, then we're not insuring you."

But luckily we solved that problem the following year in 2000 when we went back down to Daytona and hooked up with a dealership named Pompano Pat's. The Pompano Pat's folks sold new and used motorcycles, and we entered into a deal with them where they would represent our brand of bikes. It turned out to be a win–win deal for both the dealer and us. They sold tons of our bikes to their customers, and not only did they help us out as dealers, but they also had the connections to get us a manufacturing license pretty easily—a huge coup for us. Even though we weren't Ford or Chevrolet, we started building bikes for dealers, and we became legitimate manufacturers.

After we got back from Florida, there was amazing news waiting on the doorstep. *American Iron Magazine* had picked Orange County Choppers as one of the top ten builders in the United States. That was a big deal. OCC was taking off fast. We now knew we had hot bikes—and so did a bunch of other builders out there. But we had something most people didn't have—more brawn than brains. We had the brawn to build our first bikes out of the gate. Nobody else was stupid enough to do that. A sane builder would make them one at a time, or do preliminary drawings. But building and fabricating a first batch of bikes in one bold collection—well, nobody else had the stupidity to do that.

We did it because we believed it would work. We had no plan. We had no projection. Nothing. At that time, it wasn't about taking risks. Judging from the looks on the faces of the people when we rolled out our bikes, we were convinced that we were on to something.

The bike that many believe launched the OCC theme bike juggernaut. Paulie photographed the Spider Man Bike across the street from the OCC Stone Castle Road shop. (Photo: OCC Archives)

VISIONS OF OCC: DO THE RIGHT THING, THEN THE RIGHT THINGS HAPPEN

SENIOR:

Our gas-guzzling motor home and wobbly trailer made it up to South Dakota for the sixtieth annual Sturgis Motorcycle Rally in 2000 without any catastrophes. Sturgis, held each August, is the largest motorcycle gathering in the United States. As at Daytona, we got decent attention from industry insiders, although we got back-shafted again as far as location. There were the usual hotdog bike builders in attendance, and they had nice setups central to everything, while we were way out on the back forty with our little trailer. We had dues to pay as low men on the totem pole.

As we approached the Sturgis event, the magazines were giving us our props, including a piece about us in a Scandinavian motorcycle magazine. You can tell the difference between the foreign and American photo layouts. The foreign motorcycle magazines have thicker and higher-gloss paper stock, larger pages, and more vivid colors. Although I can't understand what the hell they've written in the articles, the layouts look cooler.

While it's probably no different in any other industry, there's this wide-scale thing going on in the motorcycle world about jealousy. It runs very deep, and it's all very macho. We Teutuls consider ourselves nice down-to-earth people, but Sturgis had an ultracompetitive vibe. While it's true that everybody has an ego and we're all in there trying to outdo the next guy, there seems to be a lot more resentment and suspicion among bike builders than you'd find in most people. Among our contemporaries, we got mixed signals. Some fellow builders were impressed by what we were doing, some didn't like us, and some admired our hot bikes but wouldn't dare admit it to our faces.

The main thing I remember about going to our first Sturgis as Orange County Choppers was an incident that, at the time, didn't seem so crucial, but later on proved to be pretty decisive in the history of our company. We found ourselves at a moral crossroads. A major bike magazine—and I won't say which—approached us with an interesting opportunity. These folks wanted us to come along for a ride with a group of other bike builders. They were going to do a slick five-page spread on everybody. It was like a big sales pitch, and it would be free advertising and give us more valuable exposure. The photographer was standing there as the guy from the magazine was running it down for us. Now, this magazine prominently featured bikes with scantily dressed and semi-nude models. They wanted to know if we were in or out. Paulie told them we needed to talk about it and would get back to them.

"What are we going to do?" I asked Paulie.

It was a shoot with the top builders, and at the time we weren't that well known. So to be in with these guys was good, and to be seen with our peers was valuable. This was at a time when we had six or seven bikes to sell that we'd brought up with us. We needed to sell those bikes, and we had an opportunity to feature them in a top magazine. Just the publicity was worth quite a bit.

"I don't think we should do it," Paulie said.

When we first started Orange County Choppers, we vowed we would not associate our bikes or ourselves with anything having to do with alcohol, tobacco, or nudity. I had my past problems with alcohol and drugs, and I think cigarettes are bad for you. My ex-wife had given Paulie and my other children a solid Christian upbringing, which Paul Jr. in particular took very seriously.

"We're not going to do it," Paulie repeated. He seemed very adamant about it. I had Paulie's back on this one, so to speak, and went along with him, although I might have been more inclined to just say the hell with it and do it. I read this magazine. I had copies in the huge stacks I kept back at home.

When the photo editor called us back, we told him we were not going to go out on the shoot. The magazine did it regardless. It wasn't like we had put an end to the whole thing. But our decision was rooted in values we forged for the company early on. It wasn't so much a biker thing. We just knew that it was wrong for us when it came down to what we hoped to accomplish for the company down the road.

I remember it being a big deal for Paulie, so I listened to what he had to say and deferred to his judgment. Making those decisions related to alcohol, cigarettes, and nudity meant us staying out of some fairly high-end bike magazines that would have made a big difference at the time. As we struggled through the first two years, starved for any press exposure and going everywhere and doing almost anything to spread our name, whether it was a waste of time or not, at the core we maintained our moral standards and swore that we would not do certain things.

"If we do the right thing," Paulie said to me, "then the right things happen. Moral values and knowing that we gotta do the right thing is important." Taking such a tough stand that day ended up making a huge difference later on, especially when we entered our next realm of bike building, which would revolutionize the course of OCC. A year later, in 2001, Paulie drew up plans for what was to be our very first theme bike, the Spider Man Bike, which caused quite a splash for us.

When we started planning that bike, it was at a time when we weren't in high demand. We were in a bit of a lull. We were even taking customers' Harleys and customizing them. The Spider Man Bike was a side project that Paulie was working on. He got the idea to fabricate spiderwebbing around the bike: chromed wheels with a spiderweb pattern, spiderweb fenders, and a spiderweb sissy bar. Then it came to him that since it was going to be a spider theme, why don't we just add a Spider-Man paint job to the mix?

Paulie spoke to Nub at Nub Grafix in Orange County about it. With this intricate, chrome-plated spiderweb fabrication covering the bike, we could have added Spider-Man on the tank, swinging between two buildings. Paulie decided to integrate Spider-Man into the bike and use the blue and red colors of his costume, but at the same time not be so obvious about it. It would be a more subtle integration of design. Paulie wanted to pull off the theme from front to back, which is why he opted for the Spider-Man eyes on the tank artwork, instead of a full-blown comic-book image like we did with the Frank Frazetta tank on the Yellow Bike.

If you look at a custom motorcycle from a distance, going down the road, it looks like a regular bike. When you view it close up, you see more and more. That's one of the cool things about visiting our bikes at shows: The longer you study them, the more you'll appreciate. The one thing a bike needs—and this is what Paulie understands—is that there has to be a line and a flow. That's the thing you have to be careful about. You can hang a lot of stuff on a bike—spiderwebs, fancy carburetors, anything—as long as it flows. Once the stuff you add breaks the lines of the bike, then it looks like crap. If you have a simple bike with the wrong seat, the wrong handlebars, the wrong headlight, then it doesn't have that right line composition. The most demanding thing about bike design is that the whole thing has to flow. And the flow is present not only on our bikes, but on the original OCC logo that Paulie drew, too.

The Spider Man Bike was the first bike that Nub painted for us. Our rider friends around Orange County raved about Nub and urged us to hire him to do our painting. It was "Nub this, Nub that. He's the best graphic guy. You need this guy." While George at RMS could do nice flames, that was about all he could do for us. Nub was young, eager, and extremely hip, and could get as crazy as we needed to get.

The Spider Man Bike was the very first theme bike we built. We rushed to get that bike done for a show in San Jose, California, that we were invited to attend. It was the 2001 Custom Chrome dealer show, which, at the time, was a huge event. A wide mix of people from all kinds of different aftermarket and parts companies planned on being there. Custom Chrome is a vendor that sells to builders—frames, fenders, any accessories and parts you needed to buy to put a custom motorcycle together. We did business with Custom Chrome after opening OCC in the steel shop downstairs and were buying quite a bit of stuff from them. As a result, we got invited to the show in San Jose because they saw that we were just making a name for ourselves. I was telling the guys from Custom Chrome that we wanted to bring out this bike that Paulie was building called the Spider Man Bike. I warned them. It was off the hook.

It became another major turning point for OCC. It put us in a position to roll out our secret weapon with all the other builders in one building. The top guys were showcasing their stuff. Jesse James. Paul Yaffe. Roger Bourget. At the time, *Motorcycle Mania* on the Discovery Channel had showcased Jesse on two highly rated shows, and everybody at the convention knew who he was. He was a big deal for the custom motorcycle crowd. I remember when he first showed up inside the building and everybody just gazed at each other and said, "Oh wow, look, there's Jesse James." After Jesse James did the *Motor Mania* shows in 2001, he was like a god. He was the first custom bike builder who couldn't walk anywhere because everybody was chasing him. He and his company, West Coast Choppers, are credited by many of us with taking custom bikes past the Pro Street look and on to the full chopper craze. He's a very talented guy who builds fantastic bikes. While the rival builders tried to be too-cool-for-school about Jesse and didn't want to give another builder his due no matter what, there were plenty of nonbuilder fans in attendance who made a major fuss over him.

We hired a guy to drive our bikes cross-country out to the San Jose Convention Center, where we met him the day before the show started. The organizers from Custom Chrome took one look at the Spider Man Bike and agreed with what I'd been telling them on the phone. It *was* off the hook. They liked it so much, they decided to place it on display right at the front entrance.

We pulled into the show with about eight bikes. There was a main dock area where the builders loaded in their bikes. When we wheeled the Spider Man Bike off the truck, people were ogling. *What the hell is that?* It had eyes on the tank. It was webbed all over with fabricated steel. It was a full-blown chopper with an extended chrome front end. It looked like a superhero. Nothing else at the show even came close. When we brought the bike into the convention center, past a bar where the builders were hanging out, you could sense how intimidated they were. It was the way the whole bike looked. There was a lot of fabrication and imagination, and it represented a whole new element in bike building: It had a theme. Nobody had done that, or at least not that we knew of. Paul Yaffe had built a bike for the Arizona Diamondbacks baseball team, which was nice. The seat was a baseball glove. Still, it wasn't as over the top and obvious as a theme bike.

Anybody from the age of three on up who walked by the Spider Man Bike could identify with it. Spider-Man was the top comic-book (and now movie) superhero. Everyone could relate to him. The bikers who brought their kids along to the show converged on our bike. It had a magnetism all its own. If you saw it, you were immediately attracted to it. Like a spider with a fly, it drew you into its web. It was the talk of the show.

"Who are these Orange County Chopper guys? Are they from Southern Cal?"

"No, you tool. We're from Orange County, New York!"

We set off a spark in the industry. People from the West Coast to the East now knew we were the real deal. People talked about us through the whole three-day weekend of the dealer show. That bike had mass appeal. Some of our competitors had a hard time with it, which I could understand. They felt slighted. Some of these people had been slaving over the mallet and torch for twenty-five years, and they had nice clean bikes. But here we were, becoming hugely popular over this one novelty theme bike.

We tried to mingle and be friendly with the other builders, but it was just like our first Sturgis. People were standoffish because who the hell were we? That was the position a lot of the builders took. We hadn't been around long enough. Having said that, I believe people felt threatened by us because we had nice stuff.

For example, I remember the first time I met this one guy, a champion of one of the Biker Build-Offs. I was in Cincinnati at a show on my own with my bikes, and somebody from *Hot Rod* magazine brought him over and introduced him to me. At the time, we were selling bikes for about twenty-four thousand dollars apiece, while he was getting about forty grand. He looked up and down at our bikes, didn't look me in the eye, sniffed, and just walked away. I felt like grabbing him and ripping his face off. I just can't stand that brand of arrogance.

After the San Jose Custom Chrome show, no matter where we took the Spider Man Bike, it was a major draw. When the people at Marvel Comics first found out about it, they were annoyed. They hadn't heard of us and were distrustful about us using their trademark comic character. Later on, after we became well known, they took it as a compliment and suggested we do *more* theme bikes based on their comic superheroes.

We weren't trying to sell the bike, though we needed the money. We were in the same dilemma as a lot of painters and artists. Once we created something amazing, we didn't want to give it up. I'm like that today. We build bikes for people, commissioned bikes, and then we don't want to give them up when the time comes for delivery. We try to keep as many of our bikes as we can. And we do.

The hip-hop pop star Wyclef Jean ended up buying the Spider Man Bike. We were selling some choppers to some guys in New York City, and they were telling us how much he wanted that bike. Apparently he had seen the bike on our Web site, and though it wasn't for sale, he came up to the shop—and we wound up selling the bike to him. It was like when we sold the Hot Rod Chopper; it was the stupidest thing we did. But, damn, we needed the money at the time.

And that's how the whole theme bike craze started. In the motorcycle world, that's what we do and what we're known for. Some people don't like us for it. They find our theme bikes to be cheesy, and everybody is entitled to their opinion. If they're hard-core riders, then in their eyes, we make fluffy cake bikes. Yet some of the builders were responding out of jealousy because of the attention we got.

The idea to build theme bikes brought the masses to us. It's what made us who we are today. Paulie was the first to suggest doing it, and a year and a half later it became a powerful business model. It still is. Today we build theme bikes for many of the top corporations. They use them as marketing tools to gain worldwide exposure and to boost employee morale. Organizations like Snap-on Tools. Airgas. Miller Electric. Gillette. Caterpillar. The US Army. And many others. All theme-oriented bikes.

The first theme bike that we got paid for was the TrimSpa Bike for a weight loss products company. We'd built the Black Widow Bike, another spidey bike, and unveiled it at the Javits Center at a huge bike show. Hundreds of thousands of people attended that show. A lot of production bikes were being shown. Harley was there. Honda, too. Our Black Widow Bike was a huge attraction, one of the hottest bikes there.

The man from TrimSpa was looking around. He was a very smart guy. He had already sponsored a TrimSpa race car, and when he saw our bike, he asked us if we could make his company a bike that would match the race car. We quoted him a price of $150,000, and haggled with him. That much money for a bike was unheard of in 2002; nobody got 150 grand for a bike. He agreed. He was our first corporate build,

The people's paparazzi go gaga over the Gillette Bike. (Photo: OCC Archives)

and he ended up getting quite a bit of exposure, which is why these companies do it. It stretches their marketing dollars, after which they tour the bike around the country for years. Then we did bikes for Snap-on Tools and Miller Electric. And we were off to the races.

Not all theme bikes are purely corporate. Some have a deeper meaning. We brought out the Fire Bike at the Louisiana Bike Expo, and there was a whole group of veterans there. A bunch of them expressed to me how grateful they were that we'd created the Fire Bike as a salute to America's firefighters. They seemed pretty emotional about it, and it flashed on me to create the POW Bike, which is one of our most famous choppers.

I figured I'd do a high-up chopper. We built it as we went along. There was no fixed plan. I made the wheels with barbed-wire spokes, and the front end was made with coins from the Vietnam era and the Iraq wars. It spanned different conflicts. Although its focus was on the Vietnam War—because that's the era I came from—it was a tribute to every fighting soldier out there. After we finished it, Paulie and I brought it to Washington, DC, where we led the annual Memorial Day motorcycle run to the Vietnam Veterans Memorial Wall. It was a heartrending moment for us, leading that pack of vets. Later, we took it up to the US Military Academy at West Point.

One of the most striking bikes we did was the Statue of Liberty Bike. A company called Gold Leaf Corporation had restored the Statue of Liberty, and when these folks commissioned us to build the chopper, they gave us some copper parts from the statue that they couldn't use. We melted them down and used them as part of the bike's mirror-gloss copper coating. What they wanted to do was build a bike that paid homage to the statue, and then create a charitable program to raise money. The bike later went on tour with country star Tim McGraw.

One of Paulie's finest chopper designs was the *I, Robot* Bike. Discovery had a deal with Twentieth Century Fox film studio, and the plan was to promote the movie by doing a bike build on *American Chopper*. With only hours to spare, we finished the bike and trucked it out to Los Angeles to be part of the movie's red-carpet premiere. We flew out, too. Will Smith loved the bike, and we had a great night posing for pictures, and watching the beautiful, sexy movie starlets sitting on the *I, Robot* Bike and getting photographed by the paparazzi.

Corporate theme bikes were not an easy field to get into. A lot of these companies will not affiliate themselves with just anybody. They do very little co-branding, and you must be extremely legitimate and on the level for them to work with you or even give you the time of day. That's why it was so important when we held the line against aligning our bikes with companies involved with alcohol, tobacco, and naked women. When we took our stand at Sturgis back in 2000, it made all the difference in the world in our ability to later attract top clients who trusted us to represent their products or services through one of our theme bikes. It was like Paulie had said earlier:

"Do the right thing, then the right things happen."

Reflections of Michael Joseph
Teutul, better known to millions of
American Chopper viewers as Mikey.
(Photo: Martin GM Kelly)

MIKEY IN THE MIDDLE

MIKE:

Before I joined Orange County Choppers in early 2003, my life sucked. I was aimless, listless, hopeless, and working at my father's former company, Orange County Ironworks. I was truly unhappy, not because of the work itself— I actually enjoyed aspects of ironwork—but because I hadn't figured out what I wanted to be. Since graduating from high school—and flunking out of college— the only thing I had figured out was what I *didn't* want to be: busboy, movie theater employee, bouncer, construction worker, and now ironworker. I installed railings in residential areas, put up support columns for backyard decks, and called in sick as often as possible, sometimes for weeks at a time. I was twenty-five years old, and miserable. I'd always been more interested in being creative than being industrious, but it seemed impractical to pursue anything like that. There is nothing worse than waking up every single morning and knowing you're not on the right track. So I did what I did best: I got myself fired. After two years of being a complete and total deadbeat, my brother Dan had to let me go. So it was time for another job.

Once I pissed away the little money I had on beer and movies, my dad reluctantly gave me a job at OCC, answering phones and taking out the trash. It wasn't particularly interesting, or challenging, but I knew it could be fun, and it was a job. I still didn't know what it was that I was good at, though, or what I wanted to do. I think a lot of people can relate to that feeling, or maybe I was just a late bloomer. But once high school ended, my friends all seemed to know exactly what to do next . . . while I didn't have a clue.

I'd always loved learning, but didn't do well in a classroom environment. Okay, that's understating the case. The truth is, I graduated eighth from the bottom in my class. It wasn't laziness; I just wasn't good at tests . . . or homework. But I really did want to learn, so I took my impressive GPA all the way to Orange County Community College. I had big plans to study my favorites, like American history and film. (I even took a television production class, unaware of the role TV would play in my future.) Sure enough, my college career proved to be even more disastrous than my high school career, and I had flunked out by the first semester. I just didn't seem to fit into the mold, which was an aggravating theme in my life.

Growing up, I felt like the black sheep in my family. I was born in 1978, and was the youngest of three, all boys, until my sister came along four years later and demoted me to "middle child" (to this day I still resent her for it). Although my parents didn't show favoritism, I felt that my father and my oldest brother, Paul, along with my mother and my sister, Cristin, had the most in common and the strongest bonds. Being a middle child was good and bad. I felt like I didn't have a defined role in the family, but at the same time, it allowed me to be more of an individual.

Over the years, I was alternately ignored and tortured. And teased relentlessly. This is typical in families, I know, but I had a disadvantage: I was born with a large head. A very large head. To quote *So I Married an Axe Murderer,* it was like "an orange on a toothpick." Eventually I grew into it, but for years my brothers and sister teased me mercilessly. It sounds trivial, but when you're a kid, these things matter. So I figured out how to survive: by making jokes. And that's how my role in my family became defined. My brothers had sports, my sister was good in school, and I made everyone laugh, even when there was tension. Especially when there was tension.

When my father first moved to Montgomery and started his steel shop, he had a reputation as the town drunk. Local officials didn't relish having his shop in the center of town, because he and his crew would make all kinds of ruckus. In essence, they were a bunch of crazies on the job, and they liked to have a lot of fun. They'd light off acetylene bombs and get into car crashes. At the time, my dad was drinking his Black Velvet. Every day and every morning, I'd hear him wake up and swear he'd never drink again, but by ten o'clock that morning he'd be boozing. It's one thing to drink like that, but to continue working as long and as hard as he did while he drank—well, I believe you have to have something wrong with you.

He'd go from point A to point B, fall down the whole way, and just keep going. It was amazing. He would drive home from a job at the Jewish Community Center and sideswipe a row of parked cars. Nowadays if you drive drunk like that, you go right to jail. Back then, he didn't get in much trouble. I think there was only one cop in the town, and my father probably drank with him. Plus, people had a different attitude toward alcoholism. Town drinkers were often viewed as cute characters. There were no such things as rehab centers, so it was a night in jail to dry out a little and then he'd be on his way.

My father had motorcycles around the house ever since I could remember. I recall the sound of him cranking up his Harley-Davidson in the garage just below my parents' bedroom. It was frightening and awesome at the same time. I'd be up there with my mom and it would be unbearably loud. I don't think she liked him riding motorcycles, for the sheer danger. When I was a kid, my father used to take me out for a ride on the back of his motorcycle. My head was so big, he had a special helmet that he'd yanked the stuffing out of so I could fit into it. It was red, white, and blue, just like Evel Knievel. It was the coolest helmet, and we cruised around on his bike, watching people stare at us when they heard the loud blasting pipes on his '74 Harley.

My father didn't hang out with loads of bikers. He'd go out on a few charity poker runs to show his bikes. He'd win best bike for the poker run, especially in the late 1990s after he started working on his motorcycles in his basement.

I think I inherited my sense of humor from my father. He has the sickest sense of humor. When I was too young to go to church, and my father was drinking, he and I would sit around and watch *The Little Rascals* and *The Three Stooges.* That whole 1930s slapstick style of comedy has always been funny to both my dad and me. We also love to laugh at the things you're not supposed to laugh at. For instance, it's hysterical when the two of us watch some person slip on the ice. We can't keep from bursting out laughing at others' (and our own) emotional and physical pain.

Being the youngest boy, over time I've had a different relationship with my father than either of my brothers. I don't turn the screws on him or piss him off as much as Paulie or Dan. Even today, I get away with a lot more because I appeal more to my father's sunnier side. As a result, I'm able to dodge his anger. If he gets mad at me, it's about stuff that didn't matter anyway. Plus, I prefer to let him think he can have his way when it comes down to serious matters that concern him. More important, he knows that I'll always be a dreamer. Like him.

At eighteen, I had no direction. I worked for Burger King for a couple of days, which went okay, but I stuffed myself with Chicken Tenders and got sick of it. Plus, I was on the cleanup shift at the end of the night, scrubbing the grease off the kitchen equipment. Sheer hell. Next I pumped gas at an Exxon station down the street from my house in Montgomery. That wasn't so bad. At nineteen, after I dropped out of community college, I threw in the towel and went back to work for my father at the steel shop. That's when the sons worked together, and things became so intense between me, my father, and my brothers that I decided a radical change of scenery was best.

So I moved to Arizona. I had a buddy I went to high school with whose cousin was a golf pro in Scottsdale. It seemed as good a place as any, and besides, it was warm during the winter in the Southwest. My buddy and I drove across the country in a Mustang and ended up finding a place in Tempe. Other than being on vacation with my family, this was the first time I had been out of state, out on my own.

I needed money quick, so I took the first job that came up. I went to work as a telemarketer selling Nokia cell phones and some discount calling plan. I was horrible at it. I hated being one of those guys who call people like you at home during dinnertime. I felt like such a burden, I didn't make a single sale. I lasted three days.

I quit that job and went straight to being a bouncer at a bar called Maloney's in Tempe, three blocks from where I lived, and since I didn't have a car, it seemed okay. I worked six hours a night and stood outside next to the front door with an earpiece and made sure nobody came into the bar who wasn't supposed to. If things had gotten extremely rowdy, I don't know what would have happened. As a bouncer, I lasted less than a month.

For the majority of my time in Tempe, I worked as a busboy at a New York–style delicatessen, bakery, and restaurant called Chompey's. It was across the street and down the road from my apartment. I was treated like crap as a busboy, and the servers were frat boys and sorority girls. I didn't get along much with them, and since they were just as broke as me, they didn't pass on tips worth a crap. So I barely made money there.

I found a job at a movie theater as an usher, doing everything from concessions to cleaning the aisles and ripping tickets. It was a small art house, and I liked selling popcorn and watching the movies. It worked out for a while, but I didn't make enough to support myself. Still, I did see quite a few great foreign flicks.

If I didn't have money or a job for a few weeks, I had my father to fall back on. He wouldn't send me a huge check, but he would send me enough to make my rent and buy groceries. While I felt ashamed depending on my dad, I'd take the money.

After four gigs in six months in the Arizona sun, I decided that was it. In 2000, I returned to upstate New York and crawled back to work at the Ironworks. Paulie and my father had just started building bikes together. I stayed on at OCI for two more years, working out in the field. In the summer of 2002, I shared an apartment with a buddy up in a small village called Wallkill. It was across the street from a bar—bad idea. I was starting to drink a lot, but I was also very aware of what drinking could lead to. After all, I'd watched my dad. I was by now out of touch with him and Paulie. I'd see them here and there, but I didn't feel like hanging out.

When my ass got canned from the Ironworks, Paulie and my father reluctantly gave me the job at the bike shop. Being the youngest Teutul son worked in my favor. I knew how to use humor to defuse family tension, which came in handy working with my dad and brother.

Pretty soon, my father yanked me off phone detail at the shop. No more would I be talking to the customers, listening to their shipping problems or taking their orders for parts or merchandise.

My life was about to take an unexpected turn. I was still just a turd in mesh shorts, working with my dad and brother in the family business, but soon my life would be broadcast into the living rooms of millions of homes. God help us all.

CHAPTER 12

The on-camera Teutul lineup filming a trailer for the American Chopper series. (Photo: Martin GM Kelly)

"WE AIN'T DOIN' THAT": THE REV, ROAR, AND KICK-START OF *AMERICAN CHOPPER* SENIOR:

The story behind *American Chopper* is pretty basic, with a simple beginning. Craig Piligian, our executive producer and CEO of Pilgrim Films in Los Angeles, was in Washington, DC, doing some small projects for the Discovery Channel. He'd just gotten back from Africa after producing *Survivor 3*. He went to lunch with Sean Gallagher, who was then the director of development at the Discovery Channel.

"Jesse James and *Monster Garage* are doing pretty well," Sean told Craig. "I'd like to find an East Coast bike builder. If you can find one, let's do a pilot."

Craig had never done anything with motorcycles, but he figured he had a knack for spotting unique talent for television.

"My background with *Survivor* involved finding good characters," said Craig, "and I was pretty good at it. Maybe I could find someone who might be interesting for television."

The first thing Craig did was jump on the Internet and look up every bike builder from Miami to Maine. He pulled information and candidates off the Net and scoured résumés, pictures, and Web sites until he narrowed the field down to about twenty different bike builders. Then he and his staff made phone calls and narrowed that list down further to ten. Included in that group of ten was us, the Teutuls at Orange County Choppers.

We weren't Craig's first choice for the pilot. His first choice was some bike builder up in New Hampshire. They talked about a creative approach, and Craig decided to do the pilot with him.

A deal was hammered out as Craig wrote up his proposal for the pilot. They were going to go to a junkyard with this guy, pull out an old bike, and refurbish it to make it look great again. Craig kept in touch with the guy in New Hampshire to make arrangements for a crew to come film the pilot. He never met personally with the builder, but he worked out the preliminaries over several phone calls. But by about the fourth phone call, Craig got a gut feeling: a bad feeling that he had picked out the wrong guy.

"The conversations I was having with the builder from New Hampshire weren't going well," said Craig. "He wasn't into it as much as I needed him to be. He lacked the passion I was looking for in a character and a bike builder. I could hear it over the phone. I looked at the pictures of his work. The bikes he built weren't the problem. It was more in his voice."

Not having met the guy face-to-face, Craig was in a bind.

"All I had to go on was my gut, his voice, and what I heard coming out of his mouth. It wasn't what he was saying; it was *how* he was saying it. His inflection. His tone. Something went off inside my brain. Something was wrong. That was on a Tuesday, and we were supposed to start shooting the show on Friday. I had a crew launched and ready to go on Wednesday. But that night, I'm still thinking I've got the wrong guy."

Craig had taken home the file with the other bike builders' information in search of other candidates. He called Sean Gallagher to drop the bad news.

"We've got the wrong guy."

"What are you talking about?"

"We've got the wrong guy."

"We're shooting on Friday, Craig. We're starting production."

"Trust me, we've got the wrong freaking guy. Go with me on this."

There was silence on the line.

"Then who else have you got?"

Craig told Sean to go to a Web site, www.orangecountychoppers.com. "Look at these two guys, the Teutuls," he said.

Sean punched up the Web site. He saw the pictures of Paulie and me and liked what he saw. We were unique looking, to say the least. Then he looked at our bikes and read more information on the site.

Craig informed Sean that a few weeks before, somebody from Pilgrim Films had talked to us. Now he was going to call us back to see if we were still interested in doing a documentary for Discovery.

The way I remember it, after we got the original call, we heard nothing for weeks, months. We figured, *Well, we've been screwed again.* We were getting ready to go down to Daytona and didn't want to drive our bikes down, so I went out to look into a service that would transport our bikes south. While I was out, I got a phone call from Paulie. He told me that he'd just spoken with someone again in reference to that documentary, a producer, and he wanted us to possibly do a show on East Coast builders. I thought, *Hell yeah!* They wanted to use us after all. Unbelievable. So Paulie and I decided we would talk about doing a one-off, one-hour documentary with Discovery. That was it.

Eight thirty on a Wednesday morning, Craig Piligian called me from his kitchen in Southern California. Paulie and I both got on the line.

"We grunted at each other for a while," Craig remembered. "We sounded like three freakin' bears in the woods, sorta talking, but mostly grunting."

"Wanna do the show?" Craig asked us. "I'd love to do it with you guys. If so, we're leaving today. We start the shoot on Friday. I think it'll be a great show. It'll be on the Discovery Channel. Are you guys interested? In or out?"

They wanted an answer immediately.

Paulie nodded. "Come on down," I told him.

I guess I was smart enough to realize that an opportunity like this comes but once in a lifetime. If a guy calls you and says he's going to put you on TV, you say yes.

"Once I heard yes, I said good-bye," said Craig. "After Senior said yes, I just put the phone down. Not *Are you sure, because we're coming down?* Not *Are you sure you have the time?* Not *Do you want to change your mind?* None of that. Just, 'We're coming Friday. See ya.'"

After we agreed, Craig said thank you and assured us that the crew would call us when they landed. Boom. Done. End of story. That was it. One quick phone call. Craig then phoned Sean back at Discovery and told him we were the new stars of *American Chopper.* After that, he called his crew and told them they weren't going to New Hampshire. They were headed to Orange County. Not Orange County, Florida, or Orange County, California. Orange County, New York.

Once the film crew got up here, they laid out the creative plan for the show. Up to that time, we hadn't discussed much of anything about what we'd shoot.

"The plan is, we're going to go to a junkyard to get a bike and—" the producer began.

"What the hell?" I said. "We ain't doin' that."

The original premise of the show was to find an old frame and build a bike out of it. We kind of agreed until they actually came down. Then we pulled a switcheroo on the crew. We told them, "No way will we build from an old frame. We're going to build something brand new." Once they saw the hot bikes we had in the shop, the Spider Man Bike and a bike I'd just built, a real nice chopper, they agreed. Besides, Paulie had a brand-new idea, a theme bike. His next project was to build a Jet Bike for himself, in honor of his grandfather, Paul S. Leonardo, who'd served in World War II. That became the first bike we built on the show. It worked out real good. We didn't intend the Jet Bike to be a patriotic thing. It was more like a personal statement from Paulie. But it was perfect timing after 9/11 and the wars and such.

At the time, the producer in the field called Craig back in Los Angeles: "Problem. Senior doesn't want to find a bike in the junkyard."

"What does he want to do?" Craig asked.

Vinnie DiMartino, Paulie, and Cody Connelly mocking up the NAPA Bike while the film crew rolls.
(Photo: Martin GM Kelly)

To their credit, Craig and his producer trusted our instincts. They went with the new direction for the show. In exchange, we pulled out all the stops building the Jet Bike. I think we lost money building that bike on the show. As we were working, it was hard to see where Craig and his crew were going with the filming. But we sensed a big opportunity.

Compared with today, the first pilot was shot on a fairly low budget. Nowadays we shoot in high definition. Back then, they had piss-poor lighting. They had a producer, one camera, and one sound guy. That was it. A skeleton crew, a real bare-bones outfit. We were uncomfortable. Paulie taught himself on the spot how to speak to a camera. I was awkward for the first couple of shows. We'd never had a camera in our faces, following us around while we worked.

Filming the first show was weird. I couldn't control what was happening. It was a runaway train. I was so involved in the business of what we were building, the Jet Bike, that when anything would happen, whether a camera was there or not, I'd freak out. I didn't tolerate any BS in my steel shop to begin with, and I wasn't about to change my style because of a camera crew. If it looked and felt like I was losing control, it's because I was. My main issue has always been control. I'm a control freak, and I was freaking out. It was a lot of stress having a film crew there *and* trying to get everything done right with the bike build.

The crew was around for about six or seven weeks. They filmed continuously as we went along. And that was the beauty of it. It was so innocent. No big Hollywood production. Just a small crew and some guys building a bike doing our everyday Teutul thing. Shouting and snarling. We soon forgot about the cameras. We dropped our guards. We were completely ourselves. A few weeks into it, Craig saw the footage that was sent back. He called Sean Gallagher.

"Look, I think I should tell you, we're not doing what I originally wrote up, what you submitted, and what everybody at Discovery signed off on. We ain't doin' that."

"What do you mean, we're not doing that?" Sean asked.

Craig didn't quite know what he had until two weeks of shooting had gone by. Even though it wasn't what anybody had originally signed off on, it looked pretty good.

Five weeks later, most of the footage was in. Production was going smoothly. The Jet Bike was completely built. It came out great. Looked real cool. The producers went home as Pilgrim Films started editing a rough cut for the pilot.

After viewing a rough cut, Craig saw something unique unfolding. The show wasn't just about building bikes. Yeah, we made great bikes. But the show was about something more. The Jet Bike was no longer the star. It was a by-product. What was surfacing was who Paulie and I were and what we were going through working together in the shop, trying to build our business step by step. The show was about a relationship, a father and son. That's what must have come through in the early footage. When the editing process began, Craig decided to slant the show more toward a father and son than toward a couple of East Coast builders building a bike.

"And make sure that guy yells every four minutes," Craig instructed his editor. "Throw it all in there. Every four or five minutes, make sure he's yelling at something or somebody, I don't care what he's yelling about. Just make sure he yells."

It was decided that the shock appeal of the show would be found in the arguments. While Paulie and I may have several fights days or weeks apart, the cut of the show had us going at it every few minutes. Sean at Discovery came in to view the rough cut that Craig's editors had put together. After viewing it, he sat in silence.

"This isn't about the bike," he said. "It's about the father and son. I don't know how Discovery is going to feel about it."

Let me put this in perspective. After the shoot, Craig didn't tell me what he was doing. Not a word. We had no communication with him. We thought they had all the footage they needed, but afterward they came back to Orange County and filmed some more. But for the most part, we didn't talk much about how the show was going to be edited.

We hadn't seen one second of the show in advance. We hadn't a clue what parts they were going to show. I expected they would leave the arguing on the cutting-room floor and focus on the Jet Bike. We were hoping we were going to be the next Jesse James. We saw what TV had done for Jesse, and hopefully it would do the same thing for us. This was our golden opportunity. Our big break. Who wouldn't want what Jesse James had? Fame. Respect. Plus, he was selling thousands of T-shirts. He had crossed the finish line. He was The Man.

When they sent another film crew back to Orange County for the second round of shooting, we had to go back and redo some key scenes. The original cameraman had missed half the building process. That took another few weeks. We had to reshoot more than half the original show. We redid the gas tank scene. We pulled the bike apart again. We pulled off the front end. Pilgrim Films edited the final cut of the show. Those folks had total freedom to cut the show their own way. What did we know about television? Then they sent it off to Discovery.

I doubt anybody at the network paid much attention to their new motorcycle pilot show. They probably just slotted it in. We didn't know if anyone had watched it prior to its airing.

The night the show premiered, we assumed we were going to be the only bike show aired that night. But we were wrong. We were just one of four bike shows. Besides our show, there was one with Roger Bourget and Billy Lane doing a Biker Build-Off. Then they ran *Motorcycle Mania,* a show that Jesse had previously done, and then another show about women riding cross-country.

Craig called me to tell us that the show was airing on a Monday night, ten o'clock.

"I watched the show and I didn't know what to think of it," said Mikey the next day. "I was proud and happy for my brother and father. I prayed to God that they wouldn't make total asses of themselves and become a laughingstock over a once-shown episode on a cable channel that they would never live down; that only my town watched. I remember their reaction. They were devastated with the Jet Bike episode. 'We look like a-holes.' When I saw them arguing, I didn't take it as badly as they did. I watched the first segment with my mother in the living room with Paul. I could almost see Paul's jaw drop. He wouldn't say anything, but you'd see his face getting a little tense. Then at one point it looked like he was going to throw up."

The other Discovery shows featuring other bike builders were straight-arrow biker shows. But when it came to us, it was like freaking *Leave It to Beaver* meets *All in the Family.* As I was watching that first pilot, seeing Paulie and me yell and scream at each other, I wondered what the rest of the bike world was thinking. It was a mockery. All those builders out there watching us, laughing at these two New York jackasses. Oh my God! The first time you see yourself on TV, well, that's devastating enough. But this was the real deal. Maybe too real. My screaming and yelling.

I got on the phone right away with Paulie. We started commiserating. We were going back and forth on the phone about how we wanted to kill the producer. One lousy television show had just knocked down all our years of hard work at OCC. We were ruined. We were shocked. Devastated.

I called Craig early the next morning, before the overnight ratings came out. I wanted to kill the guy. I cleaned his clock on the phone. "You've ruined my life," I screamed, "and my career. I didn't expect this." It was the same scream they had liberally inserted through the show. Only angrier. I told him I was going to hop on a plane, drive out to his studio, and give him the beatin' of his life.

"How does it feel now that you've ruined everything we've worked for over the past couple of years?"

"Wait a minute, Senior," Craig said to me. "Just hang on. We might have a great number. Wait and see what the response is. Let's see what happens." *What difference could a few hours make?* I thought. It was seven in the morning and all I wanted to do was rip Craig's freakin' head off. I was shaking as he continued trying to calm me down.

"Look. The ratings come out at four o'clock this afternoon," Craig said. "East Coast time. Try to relax. Let's see how the viewers respond. Let's see what they post on the Discovery Web site."

I wasn't buying this. I slammed the phone down on Craig.

By one or two o'clock that afternoon, we started getting calls at the shop. Nonstop. Tons of calls.

"Great show."

"Really amazing."

That day, the Web boards at Discovery started heating up. We received a flood of e-mails, too. I don't think, up to that point, we'd received a single e-mail. Now, the day after the show aired, we were getting hundreds, thousands of responses from people who loved the show, or at least related to it. Either they dug the bikes, or they had a father like me, or they related to Paulie as a son. It was incredible.

Finally I began to settle down and see the light. I was starting to sense that, besides the bikes, we had achieved something on television that hadn't been done before. A family, a father and son, relating to each other, no holds barred. The gloves were off. I was shouting. Paulie was barking back. For better or for worse, we'd been exposed, stripped naked in front of America. I knew my life would never be the same after that. We'd just experienced a tidal wave of exposure. We had no choice but to ride with it. And ride we did.

"The ratings were huge," said Craig. "Considering the time slot, I think we got maybe a 1.2 share or a 1.3 out of the box. No promotion. Discovery slapped it on the air on a Monday at ten o'clock during the dead zone. But we surprised everybody. Ultimately it was the yelling and screaming and showing the family mixed in with the bike building that made the pilot brilliant and raw."

Discovery was wondering how the hell a couple of yahoos from upstate New York had scored a 1.2, 1.3 rating share on a Monday night. They called Craig and wanted to do another pilot. Maybe they didn't believe the results from the first one. Maybe they suspected it was a fluke. So we did a second pilot with a little bit of backstory added from the first episode.

Boom. Another big number. The message boards lit up again. Our OCC Web site crashed. We didn't have enough room to hold the e-mails we were getting. Discovery was on the fence. They were moving slow. But Sean Gallagher, in his wisdom, figured out how to get thirteen more shows ordered. After everybody signed off, *American Chopper* the series was born with thirteen new episodes. If you talk to Craig or Sean, I know they'll tell you they went out on a limb. They took as big a risk as we did putting *American Chopper* on the air.

With each show, our ratings escalated. We became huge TV stars, and soon we couldn't walk the streets like normal people anymore. We were like rock stars. Much later, when we went to England, we were mobbed like the Beatles. We seemed to have come out of nowhere, and all because Craig had a gut feeling he'd picked the wrong guy.

That's how suddenly fate changes your life.

Between the two shows, I met Craig face-to-face; he flew to OCC when we got picked up for the series. At that point, he hadn't met Mikey. We were doing show number two of the first series and I was showing Craig around the business. We were sharing space with the Ironworks. Walking in, Craig saw this kid in the upstairs shop, where the steel business was at the time. It was Mikey in his short pants. It was two degrees outside and Mikey was wearing a sweatshirt, white socks, boots, and shorts, with his feet propped up on the desk.

Senior high-fives OCC's Mike Ammirati while Jason Pohl and Mike look on. (Photo: Martin GM Kelly)

"Senior, this kid, he sorta looks like you," Craig said to me. "Who is he?" He looked like he owned the damn place with his boots up on the desk.

"That's my other son Mikey," I told Craig.

Craig was stunned. "Your other son? I didn't know there was another son. We have to get him in the show."

Mikey and the bubble wrap episode started.

Nobody planned to get Mike in on the show. He got in under the wire. Four months before the show aired, I'd brought Mikey in to answer phones and sweep up. He needed a job, and I needed someone to answer the phones. They were driving me crazy. And that was Mike's introduction to the show. He got to know the film crew since he was interested in entertainment. They were going to teach him the trade. Who knew how long the show would last? So the show's original producer gave Mikey a chance to work with the sound, but, like a jackass, he kept putting the boom in the shot. It was almost like a spoof with Mikey screwing up. We soon found out that Mikey's place was in front of the cameras, not behind them.

We did go through a few production teams. It was tough for TV crews to pull up stakes and move to Orange County, but we eventually developed a skilled team led by Steve Nigg. Their guys donned our T-shirts and worked alongside us. They've figured out, as a production unit, how to co-exist inside our business because that was the only way to give the show its natural feel. *American Chopper* is a docudrama. Real people, characters, coming to work every day. The crew simply films what we do without getting too much in the way.

By 2003, Discovery had become the "wheels network." They'd gotten heavily into motorcycles, and the ratings on that stuff were pretty good. I didn't watch a lot of the Biker Build-Offs, though I've seen a few of them lately. They kind of suck because the characters are so dull.

American Chopper took things to a different level. We added character, humanity, and lifestyle, taking the approach that television viewers would be interested in us as people, and not just as bike builders. Sure, there was interest in moving parts and mechanical stuff, in motorcycle culture and in the biker way of life. But we weren't a biker family. We were your typical family-family. Except that we built bikes and argued a lot. But more important, we were an American family whom everyone could relate to—mothers and daughters, sisters and brothers, cousins and aunts, and especially fathers and sons. And that's why the show struck an immediate chord.

Part of the appeal of the show is that everything doesn't turn out perfectly. There are problems and bumps in the road along the way. Just like life. You didn't see bikes falling off the lifts on the other bike shows. You didn't see parts that failed to fit or extreme interaction between the characters. That happens only in real life. One bike falls off the lift because somebody forgot to harness it. Another bike falls off the next day. An exhaust won't fit. The show wasn't peaches and cream. Neither is life.

More important, *American Chopper* hit on the dad thing. Everyone knows what it's like to work for your dad, whether he orders you to clean the garage, vacuum the pool, cut the grass, or wash the car. In my eyes, sons can never get it right. Sometimes they need a smack on the back of the head.

I have to give credit to Craig and the show's producers for leaving that arguing in. They could have easily edited out the interesting stuff. I was looking for a polished show. That's what I was brought up watching on TV. Nice families and nice stories. But the true reality freaked everybody out. What did we know about putting together a show? Had they asked me to direct it, it surely would have been a flop.

"A television show is about the public," Craig has told us again and again. "If it strikes a chord with the public, they're going to watch it. If not, we're done. It doesn't matter if the network execs like it or not. If the people don't watch it, you're done. So we program to the people, not to executives.

"I don't know if *American Chopper* could have happened on ABC or CBS or any of the big networks. That's a good question that's been debated, and I don't know the answer.

"All I had were gut feelings, and when you have those feelings, they gnaw at you. And if you're a good producer, you go with your gut. Nothing is etched in stone. You make the necessary changes and take the risks. This was one time when the last-minute changes and risks actually paid off."

Craig often gets asked about the show's life span. How long will it last? Who knows? Soap operas can last twenty, thirty, fifty years. I think *American Chopper* could last as long as we are a family, and as long as we keep bringing in interesting characters. The show could go on for a long, long time. I hope there's an audience who, every week, wants to know what the Teutuls are up to. Or how bikes are built. After over a hundred episodes, the show draws every type of person, and not just guys who dig motorcycles.

"For *American Chopper,* we were expecting eighteen- to thirty-four-year-old males," said Craig. "But we got everybody, aged six to eighty, because we became a family show. Kids watch it. Thirty-year-olds watch it. Fifty-year-olds watch it. Eighty-year-olds watch it. The show relates across every single demographic. Female. Male.

Young. Old. Everyone. That rarely happens. I never imagined *American Chopper* would cross eight decades of demographics. But it did.

"*American Chopper* has made television history. First, it changed how people do reality television. It's one of the first docu-soaps to feature a family on an ongoing basis. *American Chopper* truly *is* a docu-soap, and I believe we've changed the face of television doing our type of programming. If *Survivor* changed the way reality television was done on the big networks, then *American Chopper* surely changed the face of cable television. Look what came after us. You can name off a hundred shows, but *American Chopper* was one of the first of its kind, aired before the tattoo parlors, hot rods, and bounty hunters."

Senior in the driver's seat at "Tanks A Lot"
in Great Britain, along with cameraman
Steve Purcell. (Photo: Martin GM Kelly)

American Chopper has its own formula as far as creating episodes goes. A typical shoot is two weeks for one hour, which is actually forty-three minutes plus commercials. The crew goes through about three hundred hours of tape for each build. The producer, Steve Nigg, talks to Los Angeles every day. They know exactly what's happening at OCC. There's a lot of communication back and forth. What are the Teutuls doing? They know if Paulie and I have just had an argument. Or if Paulie just threw a hammer. Or if Vinnie walked out. Or if Mikey started going crazy. Or if Rick got hurt. Or if we're building a bike for so-and-so, or if Mikey's going down the street to do this, or if I have a toothache. They get the full two-week lowdown on our complete schedule, and then sort a show out of it. Everybody from the shop has a certain appeal because they're all naturals in front of the camera.

Once the film goes from Orange County to LA, four or five of the best editors cut and edit the footage. They have two producers looking at and logging footage as well.

If *American Chopper* weren't edited properly, the show could be as dull as watching paint dry. But I guess we're never boring. One of the best episodes was when I had a toothache and had to go to the dentist. The editors interplayed hilarious cuts between me with my toothache and Vinnie at the drill. That was great.

I feel we've been good about letting the film crew do their thing while they let us build our bikes in relative peace. They've been very respectful. They don't tell us how to build our bikes, and we don't tell them how to film their TV show. It's about mutual respect, and they've done a good job by us. It's been an incredible relationship. Very seldom do we pick up the phone and complain how we're being portrayed on TV.

Watching *American Chopper,* you're watching the American Dream unfold every week. If you want to know about the American Dream, tune in and watch our show. That's the American Dream.

While there's been a certain amount of luck involved in our lives, we've also tried to capitalize on opportunity. If an opportunity comes your way, put everything you can into it. Some of your success might come about because of straight business sense. But to be successful at what you do, you have to put a lot of your heart into your work and capitalize on your breaks. Put 1,000 percent into what you're doing. Live it to the max. Be compulsive. I attribute our success to the same compulsive behavior I get criticized for on the show.

What happens if the show runs its course is up to us at OCC. We control our destiny. I'm sure there's going to be longevity. We don't worry about overexposure. Once a week isn't overexposure.

Discovery has aired the daylights out of these shows because they're timeless. They're a lot like *I Love Lucy,* and honestly, that's how they've been fashioned.

"When we first started up," said Craig, "we wondered, *How are we going to do this?* So we used the *I Love Lucy* model. If you look at every *I Love Lucy* show—and we've studied them—Lucy gets a job. Senior has a sore tooth. Mikey pops bubble wrap. The shop is dirty. Vinnie gets a new roof on his house. Everyone has one little plot we're following. That way the shows remain timeless and relatable. Just as you can watch *I Love Lucy* or *M*A*S*H* forever, *American Chopper* is just as timeless. You can rerun them, watch them, and find nuances you hadn't seen before. That's the mind-set we had from the very beginning, going back to the basic roots of TV.

"Other producers might sit here and run BS by you, saying how it was planned out, and that they were brilliant or that they sat and looked at every frame and nuance. But I won't do that. *American Chopper* is very simple. We looked at it. Saw that it was about the guys. Ran with the concept of a family, and that's what came of it. Fortunately, I got lucky on a Wednesday morning in my kitchen."

And fortunately Orange County Choppers said yes.

CHAPTER 13

Two Americans in Paris: Mikey and Paulie in front of the real Eiffel Tower in France (not Las Vegas). (Photo: Martin GM Kelly)

FAME, HISTORY, HEADLOCKS, AND SLAPS ON THE BACK

MIKE:

For some reason, my brother and dad thought I'd be the best one to tell you about Orange County. Maybe it's because I love history, or maybe because I love Orange County. I didn't always love my hometown. I used to think I wanted to get the hell out of it. Once the show started and I got the chance to travel all over, though, I realized that Orange County, New York, is one of the most beautiful and unique areas in the country.

Orange County is not as rural as it was when my father first moved here. Yet in the little town where we live, Montgomery, everybody knows everybody, and with its postcard scenery, it's a beautiful place to come home to. Plus, we're just sixty miles north of New York City, the greatest city in the world.

A lot of people are unfamiliar with Orange County, New York, including people from surrounding counties. But I love it. And it's got a great sense of history, which you can see everywhere: monuments, historic buildings, statues, town squares. All the streets are named for founders, generals, guys like that, and I grew up with a good sense of how Orange County came to be. I'll do my best to remember the names and dates, though all information relayed herein may not be entirely factually correct. Here goes.

Legend says that when Henry Hudson sailed up the river back in the 1600s, he pointed toward the Montgomery/Newburgh area and pronounced it a "pleasant" place to build a town. I personally think he could have done better than "pleasant," but whatever. Eventually word got out, and people moved here. Although it was indeed "pleasant," apparently the soil sucked for farming, and the settlers unsettled themselves and moved to Pennsylvania, which apparently had better dirt. But eventually, by the mid-1700s, there were churches, silversmiths, and, most important, agriculture. Apparently our dirt had gotten better. And given its proximity to the Hudson River, the goods that came out of Montgomery could be easily sent down to New York City, New Jersey, and other outlying areas.

In the last century, Orange County has boomed both agriculturally and industrially. But over the last thirty years, the farmland around Montgomery has been drastically reduced to make room for more and more housing developments.

Since 9/11, a lot of people from New York City have moved to Orange County because it's the farthest north you can live and still qualify to be a fireman or a cop in the Big Apple. Anyplace beyond Orange County is considered out of commuting range, so over the past few years, the Manhattanites have caused property values to skyrocket. Commuters can take the train into Manhattan every morning, and leave their families in the country, free from the rat race.

During the spring and summer, Orange County is a wonderful place to ride motorcycles. When I go out on runs with my father, we ride up north toward Ellenville in Ulster County, a little village up in the mountains. We cruise by a beautiful gorge, heading east to the Hudson River through winding forest roads and mountains toward the small college town of New Paltz. We might grab a bite there and head south onto flat country roads back around to Newburgh and Montgomery.

It's hard for me to believe that the Teutuls have become America's most famous bike building family. What amazes me more is while we are renowned for our choppers, we've circumvented the hard-core biker culture and taken our bikes public, right into the mainstream.

I don't consider myself a biker at all. I enjoy riding the choppers we build, and lately I've been test-riding the newer ones. Sometimes when I cruise down Route 17K, I have this fear that animals will run out into the middle of the road, or a deer will jump out in front of me, or a car could hit me. That crazy paranoia in the back of my mind only adds to the excitement of riding on an OCC chopper. I ride wearing shorts, like an idiot. I know I'm asking for trouble there.

Like my father, I prefer cruising alone. I don't like riding with lots of other bikers. If anybody wants to roar past me, I'll gladly move over. It's a hassle when some cowboy comes roaring up right next to me and cracks his pipes, trying to impress me because he knows who I am. It scares me, to be honest, and that's why I stick to the back of the pack when we go out riding.

It's true: Choppers are harder to ride than most Harleys. But they're not as difficult as you might think. It can be intimidating, stretched out with the angles and broad turning radius. While a chopper is harder to maneuver at slow speeds, once you get going, you'll find the proper balance point and cruise along happily.

Actually, I much prefer scooters to motorcycles and choppers. Scooters are lots of fun, right down to the beep of the horn. I have a little Yamaha 50cc Italian-style Vino scooter that I like to tool around on. You may remember the episode where Paulie souped up my scooter by boring out the exhaust and increasing the airflow. It's a peppy little machine now: I get seventy miles to the gallon and can park it anywhere.

People ask me why I always wear shorts. Truth is, there are quite a few of us shorts-wearing dudes out there—look at Angus Young from AC/DC, or Mario Batali, the famous Italian chef. Hey, shorts are my thing. They're comfy and part of my look. I wear them in the cold because it's not like I'm out snowmobiling or skeet shooting (one of my favorite pastimes) in fifteen-degree weather. Walking from the OCC shop to my truck to my living room in the cold is no big deal.

During the first television season, I got an opportunity to build my own bike. I chose a Blues Bike to pay tribute to the various blues musicians I love. Building the bike, I roped myself into having to learn how to ride. When we filmed the Blues Bike episode, I had never ridden one before, let alone a dirt bike or anything. So I enrolled in a course at nearby Stewart Airport, where riders get their permits, take their written tests, and then pass their motorcycle license courses in a two-day period.

The whole thing was a nerve-racking experience. I didn't know anybody in the class, and I had a five-man film crew following me around the whole time. I sucked. Everybody in the class was hamming it up for the camera, or else looking at me as if I was some big shot. When the time came for me to take the test, I knew I had the riding skills, but I got so nervous being in front of the cameras and with the people watching, I choked. I failed the test. That was no fun, especially in front of millions of viewers on television.

I've been at OCC for about five years. I've learned certain skills, but I don't know how to rebuild a motor or fabricate motorcycle parts from scratch. It's just not my thing. Mainly, I love being around the people I work with. There are so many characters at the shop. With the TV crew and the custom bike business, there's so much going on every day, and so many wild and interesting places for us to visit, from Las Vegas to Daytona to Sturgis to the United Kingdom, not to mention the bike shows and personal appearances where we're able to reach out to our fans.

Another thing I get asked about a lot are the cameras. You get used to them. I'll often forget that the cameras are on at work. We're comfortable; I don't feel uneasy thinking I'll be watched by millions of people. It's as if the cameras have disappeared. I'll come to work and there are days when I honestly feel like I'm humping a seven-to-five job—just an Average Joe going to work. On other days, I'll look around me and can't believe the magic that's happening. I have to pinch myself to find out whether or not I'm dreaming.

Yet it hasn't been altogether as easy as it looks being famous and recognizable on the street. When I'm strolling down Fifth Avenue in New York City in my black shorts and University of Michigan sweatshirt, it takes less than ten seconds before somebody inevitably yells out, "Hey, Mikey!"

OCC designer Jason Pohl and Mikey pose with their
Piano Man Spoof Bike, built just prior to a visit by Billy
Joel to OCC headquarters. (Photo: Martin GM Kelly)

At personal appearances, folks automatically flock to my father first. That's because he carries a great presence with him. His arms are gigantic. He's got this crazy mustache. I don't know anybody else who looks like the guy. The funny thing is the children's response. They love my father because he looks like such a cartoon character. So unreal. You'd think that since he's so intimidating to adults, kids would run away. Yet most children latch right on to him. It's amazing.

Being a public personality has its privileges. People don't realize how much exposure you need on a reality TV show like *American Chopper* to be considered a celebrity. The truth is, it takes a long time to develop a notoriety or cult of personality on television. I've noticed that celebrity comes in waves: It depends on how much face time you get on the tube. There are some days when you think it's dying down, then everything gets nutty again, with people honking their horns and yelling at you from the street.

All in all, people are very nice to me. But some people can be crazy. I once had a guy ask us to sign his baby, his newborn infant, with permanent markers. I thought, *What's wrong with this guy?* That's sick.

You get a lot of drunk people hanging on you, grabbing you, smacking you on the back, and putting you in headlocks. They mean well, but at the same time I want to knock some of them silly for them getting handsy with me. But then I'd get myself arrested for assault. It's strange. I don't know these people, though they feel like they know me. Courtesy and manners fly right out the window. I wouldn't walk up to you and tell you what a jerk your father is, yet people do that to me all the time. At the same time, it can be wonderful when people come up to you and say nice things, like how you helped them out in their lives, though it seems silly and absurd. I especially love the kids being so bright-eyed, asking the most honest questions about being a part of a crazy family like the Teutuls.

I need my privacy like everybody else. Sometimes when I'm in public, I just want to hang out with my girl, my niece, or my close friends. Yet people won't leave me alone. Then there are other times when it's nice to be praised by strangers. My feelings change day to day on the subject. Some days, I hate being famous. Other days, it's great. On the whole, everything seems to be working out fine. Nobody takes care of me like my family. Other times, I feel like I'm too anchored to my family.

Why the hell should I complain, like a whining little bitch? Who would feel sorry for me? You become a celebrity knowing the risks and downsides. If you don't, you're not being honest. It's not easy losing your anonymity. Privacy is a valuable commodity that most people take for granted and don't value as much as they should. For instance, if I need private time with my mom and we're having dinner in a restaurant, and somebody wants to take my picture with them, I have to draw the line. You can't cater to the public incessantly. Yet some people take no the wrong way.

At one point when I first joined the show, the fame and the craziness got out of hand and affected me negatively. Although it can be a blessing, fame is something that's very difficult to adjust to. There are certain things about fame that most people just don't understand; you just have to learn them for yourself. So I started drinking a little too much. Fortunately, my father was a powerful example. We know what happened to him, and as a result he can no longer have a drink. I kind of saw myself in him and got scared. Thank God I caught myself and cut down significantly. Again, I don't know if an alcohol problem is hereditary in my family or if it's just a learned behavioral affliction. Difficult to say. But if you ask my father, he will tell you it's a disease. Looking back, I might have been on the verge of going too far with my own drinking.

One person I've looked up to is David Letterman. He's been one of my personal heroes growing up. When we're on TV shows like the *Late Show,* I get so nervous I could puke, especially when they stick me outside doing remotes. The thing is, David likes us. I know he watches our show a lot. To be on the Letterman show and hold my own in an interview with Dave is a dream come true, a pinnacle of my life.

Besides Letterman, I'm a huge fan of Bill Murray. I love his wry sense of humor. I'm crazy about indie films like *Waiting for Guffman* and *Rushmore.* I love directors like the Coen brothers. *The Big Lebowski* is one of my all-time favorite movies. Everything Wes Anderson does—*Rushmore, The Royal Tenenbaums,* and *The Life Aquatic with Steve Zissou*—is pure gold. *Stardust Memories,* the 1980 Woody Allen movie, is the ultimate movie that best explains the twisted concepts of fame and celebrity.

Once when we were on *Live with Regis and Kelly,* Regis spoke about Don Rickles in his monologue. During a commercial break, I asked Regis, "Do you know Don Rickles?" To me, Rickles is The Man. Regis agreed. "Don Rickles *is* The Man." I think it would be the ultimate honor to be insulted by Don Rickles.

Because I am who I am on TV, some people think I'm some lovable idiot. During some Morning Zoo radio interview, a guy with a big voice behind the microphone asked me a bunch of stupid and run-of-the-mill questions, including the most idiotic one, "How does it feel being number one as the biggest dumb-ass?" I sat there speechless, then angry. He didn't even ask his stupid question politely. What a jerk. I couldn't answer. Then he asked me, "Is there anybody in the running at your shop or in the world up for being the world's second biggest dumb-ass?"

Like I said, I'd much rather be insulted by Don Rickles.

CHAPTER 14

Senior marries Paula Leonardo in 1972. (Photo: Paula Teutul personal collection)

PAULA'S STORY

PAULA TEUTUL:

Paul and I met while attending Pearl River High School soon after I moved from the Bronx and he from Yonkers. We were friends throughout high school, although he would have liked it to be more than that. Then he went into the merchant marine and I went away to college. We were two very different people in many respects. He was a character, always getting into some kind of trouble. He was a cross between a lost puppy and the kind of guy you wouldn't want your daughter to date.

We dated after high school for a couple of years and were married in 1972. My children have often asked me what I saw in him. I think he was all that I wasn't—laid-back, easygoing (not as angry as he is now), and a risk-taker. We went through a lot of hard times. The big fire when the paint vat went up in flames. A couple of partners came and went. Paul was like the Energizer Bunny. He kept going and going.

Not long into the marriage, I knew there were problems on the horizon. Something was wrong. I couldn't put my finger on exactly what it was, but, determined to make the marriage work, I took on the responsibility to fix it, although I didn't know what "it" was.

"It" turned out to be alcohol/drug addiction and all the ugly, negative, and destructive behaviors that followed. As much as Paul drank and took drugs, it amazes me that he came out of those years with anything at all—let alone the Ironworks business, his family, and his life. The ongoing impact of this situation would bring me to an emotional bottom several years later.

The motivation and driving influence to survive was fueled by my desire to be there for our three sons: Paul, age six, Daniel, age four, and Michael, age two. It became clear that Paul could not be depended on to care for them.

Slowly, I made my way back from the depths of despair with the help of God and the supportive fellowship He sent my way. I learned that I could not change others, but I could change me. I couldn't change the past or the pain it had caused our young children, but I could choose to do things differently from that point on.

As a youngster, Paulie was one to get into mischief at every opportunity. He had a smile that could light up a room and melt your heart at the same time. Consequently, he got away with a lot. When he was about three and a half years old, a friend kept him for me one afternoon while I ran errands. When I returned, the grimace on her face told me something was wrong. Paulie had gotten hold of a box of macaroni and cheese and dumped the powdered cheese into the fish tank. The fish were floating belly-up among the yellow and orange bubbles. Even at that age, he was tinkering and experimenting.

In my pain and confusion, I depended on Paulie, and soon he felt responsible for my well-being. It was time for me to take responsibility for my own happiness and allow him to be a kid again. There was something that Paulie once said after his dad got sober: While all the arguing was going on, his greatest fear was who would take care of him. It breaks my heart that he lived with such insecurity.

In 1982, two years before Paul entered recovery, a daughter and sister arrived at the Teutul home. A Polaroid photo was taken of Cristin shortly after birth so the boys could get a first look at their new baby sister. I later found out that Paulie had gone door to door showing it to all our neighbors. Maybe that is when their special bond began.

Paulie has always been wise beyond his years, with a compassion for others that is rare. I can remember him designing the OCC logo at the kitchen counter. I was with him the night the OCC logo came to be. I'm certain his creativity at that moment was divinely inspired. When I see that logo—and I've seen it everywhere—I'm reminded of the faithfulness of God and that maybe *He* has a purpose in all this that is greater than the obvious.

Danny was always the serious and responsible member of the crew. Unlike his three siblings, he was neat and tidy. He did well in school and was very competitive.

Sports were a natural for him. For a time, Danny, a die-hard Jets fan, wore only clothes with the Jets emblem on them. He was and still is a Jets fan through and through. When there was no one around to play football with, Dan would play both offense and defense. He would mimic the cheers of the crowd as he scored a touchdown and danced the celebration dance. When he played indoors, he replaced the football with a dish towel, and the routine would begin all over again. Later, after Danny was quarterback for the Valley Central varsity football team, in Montgomery, he heard a few cheers of his own from the stands.

When Danny started at Orange County Ironworks, with hard work and the sheer determination to succeed, I knew he would become a successful businessman. For a young man, Dan has great insight and will do whatever it takes to better himself and take care of his family.

Michael was and still is the most jovial and content of all. He was just happy to be part of his older brothers' lives. The advantage to their being two years apart was that they always had playmates.

An early Teutul family portrait. Left to right:
Mike, Paula, Cristin, Senior, Paulie, and Dan.
(Photo: Paula Teutul personal collection)

One hot August day when the kids were young, Mike, Danny, Danny's friend, Cristin, and I went to the local fair. The boys went off to the bathroom and came back without Michael, each thinking the other had him. We looked high and low for him: I thought I would pass out between the heat and the fear that swept over me. Finally, after what seemed to be forever, there was an announcement made over the loudspeaker that a lost boy fitting Michael's description had been found. We ran to the other end of the fairgrounds to find Mike. At that point, we were both in tears.

Shortly after that, we had planned a day trip to a water park in Pennsylvania. After his last escapade, so great was his fear that he would get separated from us again, Mike insisted on wearing a child's harness that went from his wrist to mine. Mike was about five years old at the time, big for his age. It was comical to see a kid his size attached to his mom.

With Mike, what you see is what you get. If he were able, he would share his success with everyone. You couldn't ask for a more loyal friend. He's also an amazing son who never forgets to remember me.

Then along came Cristin, who instantly won all our hearts. We had the daughter we'd longed for, and the boys had a baby sister to shower with attention and love. Although the boys will say that she is spoiled, they were doing most of the spoiling. That continued until she became old enough to tease and get a reaction from her. Although she has grown to be an independent young lady, they continue to be protective of her.

Cristin and I have had our share of disagreements—all the struggles that come with the letting-go process. I have always been overprotective of my children, and she was no different. She attended four years of college in Rochester, New York, six hours from home. I was forced to "let go and let God," and once again, He did not fail me.

It is amazing for a kid who was a social butterfly in high school to make the progress that she has over the past several years. Not only did she study hard through four years of college and earn a degree, but she also worked through some difficult situations with grace and courage. Today Cristin is working as a registered nurse at a large hospital in Rochester, New York. It would be an understatement to say we are all proud of her.

The joy my children have brought into my life was my saving grace in an otherwise chaotic life. Addiction brings with it upheaval and instability; you never know what to expect or when to expect it.

I learned early on to depend on a God who was unchanging and stable, and He has remained my rock throughout the many changes life has brought my way. It's true: Good can come out of a not-so-good situation.

There were several years in Paul's early recovery when, as a couple and a family, we worked at repairing the damage caused by those years of addiction. Things on the home front improved. We spent time together as a family attending the boys' sporting events. We spent time together during the evenings, weekends, and at church on Sundays. There was finally some sense of normality. Life was good.

During this time, after boarding the Teutul Shuttle conversion van, we took several family vacations. I don't think we ever took a road trip where we didn't, at some point, get lost. We almost planned on it. The trip always took longer than expected, especially if it was my turn to drive. We also took one unforgettable trip by train to Orlando. Twenty-four hours on a train with four cranky children and two cranky adults. What were we thinking? Because we all loved the ocean, most of our trips took us south to New Jersey, Virginia, and the Carolinas.

We soon outgrew our first house and were able to design and build a more spacious home, one where we could all spread out a little. Despite his faults, Paul was always a good provider. We never wanted for anything financially. He had, and still has, a generous heart.

By 1997, Paul and I split up. It's always sad when a marriage ends. Divorce undermined everything I believed in. It took years to get to the place within myself where I could even consider it. I didn't take my decision to divorce lightly. It was a devastating time in my life; the ripple effects can still be felt today. As Friedrich Nietzsche said, "What doesn't kill you will make you stronger."

I have mixed feelings when I see my family portrayed on television. There are many aspects of the show that I enjoy, but what bothers me most is that *American Chopper* seems to exploit the fact that Paul loses his temper. I know Paul loves his children, but I can't always understand how he can justify his behavior on the show. The outbursts have been used to improve ratings—the very behavior that has caused so many personal problems for our family. Words are powerful; they don't just bounce off. Words have the ability to penetrate deep within, especially when they come from someone you care about.

I've always known that Paul and Paulie had a love–hate relationship, but not to that extent. I knew they had issues, but I couldn't believe it had escalated to that point. Maybe it's because sometimes they are so much alike.

Paul and I have at least one thing in common: our love for our children. Still, we have different ways of expressing that love.

CHAPTER 15

Helmeted and jacketed Helen Teutul, the eternal Yankees fan, gives the all-clear, thumbs-up sign. (Photo: OCC Archives)

GRANDMA HELEN TEUTUL

SENIOR:

America knows her as Grandma Teutul. I know her as Ma. Even though my birth mother, Josie DeVito Teutul, died over twenty-eight years ago, I consider Helen my real ma. Not my stepmother. At OCC, we consider Helen Teutul the most beloved member of our family and team. We find her cheerful nature contagious. Whenever we need a boost on the television show, we bring Helen in. I hope that when I make it into my late eighties, I'm just as much of a spitfire as Grandma Helen Teutul.

Helen Blachut was born in Pittsburgh in 1918. Early in her life, she experienced some extremely tragic moments. Her mother was killed when she was just a little girl. While her grandfather was tearing down the roof of an old house to use for lumber for his furnace, Helen's mother went out to visit with one of her babies in a carriage, to bring her father some lunch. Helen's grandfather was perched on top of the roof. When he pushed the chimney down, it accidentally fell on Helen's mother and the child, killing them both instantly. Her mother left behind three little girls. Helen was just four years old. Her sisters were eight and two. Three girls grew up motherless.

Helen's father was a coal miner in West Virginia. Every time there was a cave-in at the mine, the whistles would blow and kids and families would run down to the shaft to watch the miners coming out. Back then, nobody from management could be counted on to go down and retrieve anybody stuck in a cave-in. If your loved ones were alive, they'd come walking out. If not, they were gone. Tough times, though Helen's father survived.

After Helen met her first husband, Joey Malara, she moved to Yonkers where my family lived. She was in Yonkers for thirty-five years. Living there was fine until she tragically lost both her husband and son in a single boat accident. The pair were fishing in Warwick Lake when the boat turned over. Helen's oldest son, age thirty-two, fell and hit his head. Her husband Joey, sixty-two, dove in after him. They both drowned the same day. Like I said, though you would never know it, Helen has definitely seen some hard times.

Before her husband died, Helen and Joey were close friends with both my parents, Paul and Josie. And when I say good friends, according to Helen, she and my mother were closer than sisters. My mother babysat Helen's kids. The couples bowled together and they both got addicted to pinochle, which they often played together.

On May 1, 1949, Joey and Helen were on hand at the hospital to help celebrate my birth with my father and mother. As an only son with four sisters, I soon became the apple of Helen's eye. I was her baby. I still am.

Helen loves to tell the story about the time my mother sent me out to the butcher's shop to buy frankfurters. At the time, you couldn't get them in a package. My mother told me to get eight frankfurters. She pinned a note on me. Back then, they wrapped meat up in paper and string. Of course, on the way home I got hungry and ate one. Unfortunately, they got loose, and the dogs following me got lucky as well. By the time I got home, eight frankfurters were down to two.

"What happened to the others?" my mom asked.

"That's what the butchers gave me," I lied. My mother got so mad at me. Helen laughed.

After Helen's husband died in the fishing accident, my mother got very sick and passed away. That left my father and Helen both single. Four years passed. My father asked Helen out to a bowling dinner. My sister Beverly and her husband had the tickets. Helen turned my father down flat. She didn't want to go. About a week later, my father paid Helen a little visit and pressed her as to why she didn't want to go out with him. Too many memories, Helen said, of my mom and of bowling and playing pinochle.

My dad asked her to go out again. This time, she agreed, and they hit the Monticello racetrack to watch the horses. From then on, they started going out together. It wasn't long before my father asked Helen for her hand. Helen ended up marrying her best friend's husband. But, according to Helen, it was preordained. My mom would tell Helen, "If I die, you marry Paul. And if Paul dies, I'm going to marry Joey." That was their deal. And that's exactly what ended up happening.

After my mother died of cirrhosis of the liver, and when Helen and my father decided to tie the knot, I needed to show my approval the best way I could. So I stood as their best man at their wedding. The two stayed together until my father passed away in 1992.

Before, during, and after Helen and my father were together, Helen was there for me. I had only a pickup truck to drive around town, so I borrowed her Cadillac to attend special events like weddings and funerals. Helen loved it when I'd borrow her car because she knew that when I brought it back, I returned it clean, spit-polished, and sparkling. It looked like a brand-new car.

To this day, Helen sees more good in me than anybody. She fondly remembers me as a good kid, and not the rowdy drinker I became. She felt sorry for me, a lonely boy outnumbered by four sisters.

As Helen will attest, my father was very strict with me. Very, very strict. He was strict with all us kids. She figures it's how I got to hollering, screaming, and yelling. But according to Helen, once my father asked her to marry him, she insisted on a change. "You'll have to stop hollering and screaming and cursing," she demanded. So during the first months they were together, my father never cursed her. Didn't holler. Didn't scream. He was a good husband to her.

When my youngest, my daughter Cristin, was born, and I was just getting my life back together, Helen would often take care of Mikey, Cristin, and especially Danny, whom she remembers as the Teutul who kept to himself the most. There were times when I would bring Paulie around to Helen's to straighten him out.

"Here, Helen," I'd say, "keep this kid busy." She kept Paulie for a couple of weeks. But she never put him to work like I wanted her to. Instead, Paulie and Helen played a lot of cards. They'd get up in the morning, and after a few chores, they'd play cards all afternoon. So when I took Paulie over to Helen's, it wasn't punishment. She loved the kid, although I've suspected that Mikey was Helen's favorite. Yet none of the Teutuls can do wrong in the eyes of Ma with her unconditional love.

When Helen first saw the *American Chopper* show, she swore she was dreaming. She couldn't believe what was happening to our family. Then when she first saw herself on TV, well, that took the cake. It made her only more proud of the Teutul name.

Helen has maintained a simple life philosophy: "Just be good. Don't do anything wrong because it'll only just come back to hit you in the face. Do unto others. Don't be selfish. Don't do anything you'll be sorry for." Sage advice from Helen. And that's what I shoot for. I keep my life and my formula for success and happiness as basic as Helen's.

The women of the Teutul family have been tough and strong and supportive. My ex, Paula, according to Helen, "is the sweetheart of sweethearts," a saint right up there with Mother Teresa for putting up with me all those years. When we broke up, our divorce took a toll on Helen. But she never told me what to do with my life. To this day, Paula looks in on Helen. After we parted, Helen remained like family to the both of us. And Cristin, now a nurse, keeps an eye on her health as well.

The Teutul fame and fortune have affected Helen's everyday life. It's hard for her to go anyplace without somebody tapping her on the shoulder and asking her for a hug or a kiss. With the success of Orange County Choppers and the television shows, Grandma Teutul has seen life change for the better. She signs autographs and occasionally fields phone calls from girls looking to hook up with Mikey. With all these phone calls, it looks like Helen will finally have to change her phone number and stay out of the phone directory.

As supportive as Helen can be, especially during the airing of the first TV episodes, parts of the show bothered her. When I would come to see her every Sunday, after she'd watched the show, she'd demand, "Why are you screaming and yelling at Paulie?"

I could only shrug.

"Everybody's going to hate you," she warned. "Especially the kids, they're going to hate you."

I'd tell her, "Ma, it's only a show. I'm not like that." But Helen didn't buy that line of crap for a second.

"I'm not going to say you're not like that," she once told me, "because you're really like that!" Helen could never tell a lie.

Helen tries to cover for me as much as she can, which is impossible. It's on television. But Helen admits that I might be getting better. She's right. I'm not screaming so much. I'm getting mellower with age, which would only make Helen happier.

Nothing is more important in Helen's life than her undying love for the New York Yankees.

"The Yankees are going to kill me yet," she often says when her pin-striped boys drop a game.

During baseball season, you can find her in front of the television or radio rooting for her Bronx Bombers. Clippings and pictures are tacked on the wall. Helen has been an eighty-year die-hard Yankee fan since she was a child, during the Babe Ruth days. She likes to tell us the story of Babe Ruth's funeral, and how the procession passed in front of our houses in Yonkers on the way to the Gate of Heaven cemetery in Hawthorne. Helen loves recalling how both sides of the streets were jammed with sullen New Yorkers, lined up, hands solemnly on their hearts. When the Babe passed by, they waved reverently to their fallen baseball hero.

So Helen's favorite bike is the New York Yankees Bike. When we finished building it, we called her over to meet the Yankee catcher Jorge Posada, for whose foundation the bike was built. She was so stunned meeting him, she kept calling him George.

Before she officially became my ma, I was close to Helen. Her joys were my joys. Her tragedies, my tragedies. When I first heard about the death of her husband and son, I remember standing at the bottom of her bed in shock. I cried and cried until my mother and father had to drag me into the living room. That's how deeply I felt her loss. Her Joey took me fishing on his boat when my own father couldn't or wouldn't take the time. Joey felt sorry for me, so he took me fishing many times, though he got annoyed when we'd do stupid boyish things like scream and yell and throw stuff into the water, scaring away the fish. Those were the young and innocent days that Helen looks back on. To her, there's nothing more blessed than family and health.

"I believe that the success and the fame is the final outcome of both our families. I wish Paul's parents were alive to see this. Many a time I reminisce, sitting in my chair, wishing that everybody were alive to see this. But then again, maybe they're watching it now."

When Helen became part of our lives, she told us she felt the good fortune was having two families, her own and the Teutuls. In the days leading up to my own father's death, I sat with him, and for the first time in my life we talked. Really talked. I asked for his forgiveness for everything I'd done to make his life hard. In return, I forgave him. We made our peace.

Helen was incredulous on the day she met Jorge Posada. She hugged him closely like one of her own grandsons. Then after he gave her a glove and a shirt, she knew it wasn't just a dream, that it was for real. So we took a photograph. On her way out, she made me promise her one thing. The photos that we'd taken: Could they be placed on her coffin?

"Why, Ma?" I asked her.

"So that one day I can show them to your father."

OCC fabricator Vinnie DiMartino and Paulie go way back to grammar school days. (Photo: Martin GM Kelly)

VINNIE DIMARTINO: PUNCH THE CLOCK

VINNIE:

Everybody at OCC takes to fame differently. I find it's a little tougher for me than most because I have so many responsibilities in the shop. I do a lot of work on the bikes *and* go out on the road. After the crowds and the autographs and the traveling, I have to be at work Monday morning. But I'm pretty laid-back about it, as long as I can stay busy and keep getting that paycheck at the end of each week.

In the very beginning, when *American Chopper* first caught on, we'd have to go out on the road for fifteen days at a time, going to places like Daytona Beach. Mikey and I laugh about that one. We did Daytona together for two years in a row—and don't forget that Daytona happens two times a year. There's Biketoberfest in October and Bike Week in March. Mikey and I would sign autographs at the Ironhorse Saloon, which is a real biker hangout where there's lots of drinking going on. We'd sit there and sign for eight hours a day. Then we'd get up the next morning, put the bikes out, help fold clothing, do that stuff, then go back to the Ironhorse later and start signing autographs again. We'd go loony after we did that eight hours a day, dealing with drunken people spitting on us and asking obscene questions. It was hell. Plus, I drove the rig down there, set up, put everything away, then drove back and was at work by Monday morning. It drove me nuts. That's what it was like during the first two years I worked at OCC. While we still do a lot of traveling and appearances, now we make them shorter events and we fly.

I originally joined OCC as a mechanic/fabricator. Whatever they needed, I did. I'm the guy who does pretty much everything, mechanically. Everything except paint. Painting's the only thing I don't do. I guess I don't have the patience for it. I've done sheet metal work with fenders and gas tanks. I don't enjoy that, either. Fortunately, my sidekick Rick Petko loves doing that stuff much more, although I have made more than a couple of gas tanks in my day.

I tend to do a lot of the wiring on the bikes. Not anybody can wire. It's a pretty complicated process. I also set up the wiring harnesses for other bikes. I see what needs to be done and how we're going to do it and how many fuses we're going to run. While other guys know *how* to do it, I'm the guy who knows *why* we're doing it, what we're supposed to be doing, and how to do it the *right* way.

I like the bike building process best when Rick and I work together. Then we just jump on the stuff. He knows he's going to do the gas tank. I'm probably going to do the exhaust. I start making the pipes. We help each other out. I jump on the handlebars. He'll jump on the fender. We're unstoppable.

When I first got here, there weren't that many of us at OCC. Christian Welter had just started a couple of weeks before. Then I came in. Nick Hansford was here. Cody Connelly was here before everybody. Mostly, though, the guys were assembling the bikes. The first couple of weeks, I worked with them, helping them catch up. But then Paulie had me help him when he started building the Black Widow Bike. It was my job to work on the custom-order bikes that weren't featured on the show. At one point before Rick came here, I had thirty-something orders to catch up with. Thirty bikes to build! As we've grown, we've taken on other guys to help us, rolling out bikes consistently.

I've lived in and around Montgomery my whole life. I went to school with Paulie. I've known him since we were grade-school kids. My father knew his father. My father owned a local gas and repair station right in the village in Montgomery. Paul's Welding was in the village, too. They had an account at my dad's gas station. My father pumped gas and worked on their trucks. Then they'd go snowmobile riding together in the winter.

I was in fifth grade, and Paulie was a year behind me, when he was picking on my little brother. Now, I'm a pretty laid-back guy, but I told him, "Hey, don't mess with my brother." But he kept picking on him, so Paulie and I had a fight in elementary school out on the playground, a real fistfight. I got a chipped tooth. The teachers broke it up and we both got sent to the principal's office. My little brother was so scared of Paulie that he told the principal I had started the fight. After I'd protected him! My own brother! I got into two fights in my life in grade school, and they both were about protecting my younger brother.

When it comes to Montgomery, I guess I'm biased. While I don't like the direction it's going, getting more and more populated, I've been riding motorcycles and snowmobiles around here since I was three. I'm an outdoor guy. I don't just sit inside and watch TV. When I was growing up, I was always outside. I started working at my father's gas station when I was nine, so I've always messed with bikes and cars. I've ridden my whole life. We rode out in the fields. We had so many trails around Montgomery. As we grew up, we've watched a lot of our favorite trails and fields gradually disappear.

As a rider, I consider myself to be a speed junkie. Speed as in velocity, I should clarify. The choppers we build here are laid-back and meant to look great, but I never cared that much about looking great. I only wanted to be the fastest. Speed is king. I rode sports bikes, but I've stopped doing that because there's only one way to ride a sports bike, and that's way too fast. I figured someday I was going to lose my license or lose my life. So I don't own a fast bike anymore. As far as being out on the roads and trails, I'm more of a dirt bike rider. I ride the choppers here when they let me, but I own a Honda that I ride off-road into the dirt.

I was originally an automobile mechanic before I was a bike builder. When I was a teenager, I started messing around with quads and motorcycles. I worked on cars right up until I started working here. I did high-performance work for my friends. I wasn't making that much money; I did it mainly because I loved working in my father's garage. I've been welding since I was ten, but coming to OCC has sharpened my skills.

Building famous bikes is a noble profession. I think Rick feels more of a connection and ownership to the bikes he's worked on in the past than me. Unlike Rick, I can get numb to the whole process. I mean, we've built so many bikes! I can't tell you exactly how many I've helped build, but I know it's well into the hundreds. Still, certain bikes do stand out far more than others. The Fire Bike meant so much to everybody. It was great to be a part of that. The Snap-on Tool Bike was great. I had a lot to do with the Statue of Liberty Bike. I did a lot of the design work and the water jet work for the Lincoln Bikes, making the parts fit and work. With that intense grillwork we did, I believe the Lincoln Bikes were masterpieces. It was like putting a puzzle together. So, yes, I do feel an attachment to some of the bikes I've worked on.

I guess I could say that I've been involved with nearly every single bike on the show except for Senior's POW/MIA Bike. I hardly touched that one. At the time, I was working upstairs with Paulie on another project.

As a fabricator, I like doing handlebars and exhaust systems. It's very difficult to fabricate unique exhaust systems and not make them look alike. There are only so many configurations you can possibly create. But I get a kick out of doing them because it's so much of a challenge.

I consider Junior to be a very talented designer. He's definitely the most talented designer we have here. When I think of Paulie designing, I think of the pre-computer days. Sometimes I'd be working on something, and he'd walk by. I'd ask his advice.

"Paulie, can you look at this piece for a minute? I'm thinking about doing something this way."

Then he'd say something to me that was so obvious, I was surprised I hadn't thought of it myself. That's how I see Junior: He's practical. Hands-on. He's very good at making the minor adjustments and saying, "If you just turn it a little bit this way, I'll bet you that would look awesome." And he's right.

Maybe Paulie doesn't know how to work on the new machines and computers, but he can visualize things like nobody else. That's what makes him a great designer. Plus, he is very open to suggestions. He's not the guy who says, "We're only doing this my way." He's not like that. He's eager to listen.

I remember Senior from his Ironworks days. Senior was infamous in Montgomery for his drinking, since I was a young kid. I'll tell you a story about Senior. I was about nine years old, and my buddy had a little Honda motorcycle that we rode all over the place. He broke the exhaust, and since he lived right next to Paul's Welding in Montgomery, I had an idea: "Let's push the bike over to his place and have him weld it real quick."

Everybody at the shop was drunk. We asked them to help us. There was one guy who worked there named John, and he laid the bike on its side. Then gasoline started spilling out of the tank just as he started welding the exhaust. Whoosh! The bike burst into flames, so John ran over and grabbed a fifty-five-gallon drum filled with ice and beer and liquor and everything. That was how they worked. I remember John tilting the drum over as the ice and the water and bottles and beer cans spilled all over the bike and put out the fire. I couldn't believe how much beer and liquor was in that drum. I knew from my father that they drank a lot, but that was the first time I saw it with my own eyes.

ORANGE COUNTY CHOPPERS

Vinnie pops a wheelie in the shop on his mini ATV. (Photo: Martin GM Kelly)

I enjoy watching the show. I try to watch each episode the first time it's shown. As far as Paulie and Senior go with the arguments, if you watch the show, you'll see that I'm pretty much the guy in the middle of it most of the time. I try not to let the arguing bother me, but I can't see how they don't take stuff they say to each other to heart. When they scream at each other and say those bad things, I know that if it were me they were yelling at, I would definitely take it to heart. My personal take on those two is that Paulie is a chip off the old block. Yet *he* thinks he's different from his dad, and neither of them can handle the fact that they're so much alike.

Sometimes I find the television production deadlines a little aggravating. Rick and I get the worst of it because there are so many weird deadlines created because of filming. We work and work and work until we're done. Then after we've barely made our deadline, the bike might just sit there for days. Hurry up and wait! I put my life aside, didn't go home, got yelled at, missed dinner, didn't see my kid, and the bike just sits there. That can get aggravating. In the beginning, it was "Cool, let's just get another bike done." It was fun. We were doing amazing work. Then after a while, jeez, I wanted to go home and see my wife and kid and eat dinner. Nowadays when five o'clock hits, I'm outta here because I'm just a worker who punches the time clock. People think, *Man, you're on television. You must be rich.* What are they talking about? I punch a time clock! My responsibilities are out there in the shop with the welders.

Part of the appeal of the show for me is the mistakes and the screwups. That's what makes *American Chopper* real. I try to remember rule number one: Metal does not always work the way it's supposed to. You can build and fabricate a complete bike, but when you've finished welding everything and it comes time to tear it down and send it out, that's where the uncertainty comes in. Heat and steel parts move around a lot. To do it the right way, everything should be welded and put back together again and adjustments made before things are painted, chromed, and powder-coated. That's the biggest challenge in welding: making sure everything is pinned tightly in the right spot so that when you weld it, it doesn't shift. That's when we get those errors and parts that don't fit properly.

When it comes to wiring, custom bikes are less complicated to work on than production bikes like Harley-Davidsons. There aren't as many bells and whistles. It also depends on what type of bikes we're building. A lot of our bikes are pretty simple, but then you get something like the Fire Bike or the Police Bike, which has more wiring than usual, so some do get complicated. On top of that, to make them look slick, you try to hide the wiring in the frame so you don't have any exposed wires. Harley-Davidson doesn't do that because it's not the best thing in terms of longevity. They make their bike more serviceable, which means they have manuals, and if, for instance, your starter doesn't work, then there's a set procedure you can check out. With our bikes, everything is custom.

Still, we do occasionally make multiple bikes. For instance, we actually did four Lincoln Bikes, and I guarantee you I can tell each one of them apart. Rick and I fabricated all four of them, and there are little things we did differently on each one. Though they may look the same, there are subtle differences. Because they're custom, the only thing I can guarantee that's identical are the parts that came out of the water jet.

When we build our bikes, we like to use a couple of different motors. We generally use RevTechs. They make a 100-cubic-inch and a 110-cubic-inch. It's a motor that was designed here in the United States that was sent over to Korea to be built there by Custom Chrome. Looks-wise, they're all right. We'll also use H&L, which has S&S components. Personally, I prefer a real Harley-Davidson motor. With Harley, you're using the original and not a knockoff. But everything is knocked off Harley. You pay more money for a RevTech motor because it's polished and chromed. It looks shinier, while the Harley motor is black. But regardless, every motor is built from a Harley style so it can be bolted onto a Harley frame. After a certain number of years, when the patents expire, things get copied, and that's what happened with the Harley EVO motor. Though they're not actual Harley motors, most of our motors are based on the Harley EVO design.

I find that there are a few significant differences between Old School and New School (or modern) design. I have my own definitions. With Old School, it depends on whether you want to keep it *real* Old School. Old School style means very mechanical, exposed steel. Old School bikes tend to use engines from a specific era, that is, the same ones Harley-Davidson manufactured: Shovelheads, Knuckleheads, and Panheads. The motor partly differentiates Old School, and you wouldn't dare put one of those Old School Harley motors on a sleek new modern bike. Old School generally means a skinny rear 180-size tire. Newer bikes tend to have a 240 or fatter rear tire.

New School modern is a little cleaner looking and uses more current components. It's flashier. Bikes from the 1960s and '70s were homemade jobbers. While I like the Old School style, I also appreciate the more modern. I especially like Old School looks combined with new technology. Cars and bikes are the same in that respect because, if you ask me, while you can't beat modern technology and dependability, you can't beat the character of a classic look, from the days when labor was cheaper and they could take the time to make things cool.

How street-worthy are OCC machines? We make our customer bikes complete with blinkers, high and low beam, horn, everything it takes to make them street-worthy. When a bike rolls out of here for a *customer,* it's ready for road use. It's got everything.

When I'm not working here or out scrambling on my dirt bike or racing cars, I have my own Vinnie custom motorcycle design that's in the works. I already have the motor and a tranny picked out; I'm just waiting to find the right frame. I'm doing it gradually as I have the money. It's going to have a Harley-Davidson motor with a modified twin-cam motor that's balanced and doesn't vibrate like the old ones.

(Vibration! That's the biggest enemy of bikes. It kills bikes!) The Vinnie custom bike is going to be a chopper, similar but not exactly like the Mikey Vinnie Bike we built in the first season. It's going to have the same rake construction, everything six inches up. It's going to be a Softail, something easy to ride with a functional seat so that my daughter can ride with me on the back.

One of the biggest reasons Senior became clean and sober was the birth of his daughter, Cristin. *(Paula Teutul personal collection)*

THE DAUGHTER YOU DON'T KNOW

SENIOR:

Not all of my children are subjected to the constant scrutiny of television cameras. Two faces you might not know are my son Dan and our youngest Teutul, daughter Cristin. Cristin is the smart one of the group. She moved upstate to become a nurse.

Cristin is old enough to remember my recovery and attended 12-step meetings when she was about six years old. With the other kids and the babysitters in a room nearby, she was close enough to become fascinated with the stories she heard going on in the recovery room. Maybe that's why she's a nurse now.

"People were so honest telling their stories, the stuff that most people try to hide. But by the time I was born, my family had settled down a lot. There were lots of issues, but my dad had stopped drinking. His drinking was a huge thing in my house, but it was something my brothers and my mother dealt with, not me."

Paula and I first separated when Cristin was in the sixth grade, but the separation didn't last long. We got back together and attempted to work things out. Our reconciliation wouldn't last. The summer before Cristin started high school, we split up for good, and that was difficult, especially for a teenager trying to figure things out.

"It was hard," Cristin recalled, "because I felt I needed stability at home, and I didn't have it and they couldn't give it. So you feel like everything else is shaky in your life, including who you are. When you don't have the stability of parents who love each other, it makes being a teenager difficult."

Still, I've felt that our kids, particularly as adults, became much better people because of what my wife, Paula, contributed early in their lives. She was there, because heaven knows our marriage didn't always make perfect sense.

"Sometimes I wonder how my mother and father were married in the first place. I think it's true that opposites attract. My mom has a great sense of humor. My dad has an off-the-wall sense of humor. She liked that about him, that he was a little bit crazy and funny. I could see the attraction. But they were such very different people as far as their personal values and how they handled relationships. My dad has a very difficult time communicating, as you can see on television."

Cristin was my inspiration, not only for quitting drugs and alcohol, but also for staying clean.

"I'm glad that in some way I could help, for his sake and for my family's sake. And I'm glad I didn't have to experience what my brothers did, watching him drink."

The one thing that Cristin was old enough to experience was counseling. And there was never a shortage of that in our family. Like the rest of the kids, she went along for the ride, though sometimes I suspect she got more out of it than us.

"I think it's important to have someone help you who is objective, who isn't involved in your life. We saw a family counselor for five years. That contributed to how I chose my profession as a nurse. Why people do what they do. That's interesting. I'm thinking about getting my master's in psychology. Boy, could I write a thesis about this family."

Unlike Paulie, Danny, and Mikey, Cristin didn't work with me at the Ironworks, though I remember her as a youngster in the fifth grade lending a hand as my secretary. But Cristin didn't escape having to work. Instead of having to haul steel, she took a job during high school at a nursing home, which is another part of what led her into nursing.

"I was really proud of my dad and happy that he had his own business."

As a little girl, Cristin took to motorcycles, just like the rest of my kids. And sometimes, to her mother's horror, I'd ride my little daughter around on my Harley, particularly the Sunshine Bike. She loved that bike, and that's another reason why I've held on to it all these years. Before I started seriously building bikes, Cristin saw motorcycles as a father–daughter bonding experience.

"I remember the Sunshine Bike. That was his first one, and it's my favorite. I'd go for rides all the time, though my mom didn't want me to, because I was little, about five or six years old. But I loved it! I love riding on the back with my dad. That is one of my favorite things to do with him. It brings me way back to when I was little, when he tightened the strap under my helmet. I liked that, and I make him do it. That's special to me. It reminds me of how much I love him."

Because she's the little sister and our youngest, my sons were naturally protective of Cristin. In addition to the boys, she had her mom to watch over her. But of all the family members, Paulie has remained Cristin's shining knight, her hero.

"Paulie was there to protect me. Every so often he'd beat Michael up for me. When I was younger, I thought Paulie was the coolest thing. I wanted to be with him. He felt like a real older brother, while my other brothers were more like my siblings. Maybe it was the eight-year difference.

"I know there's intensity," Cristin remembered, "and that there's been a lot of arguing through the years. If Michael and Danny were to do something, and Paulie was to do the same thing, the arguments would be way bigger with Paulie and my father."

But Cristin watched Paulie screw up, too, especially smoking, both tobacco and pot. When that went down, Paulie was rushed into rehab. Both Cristin and I wonder if, because of my experiences, that might have been an overreaction to Paulie's experimentation with drugs at sixteen. But then again, maybe not.

"My parents were very sensitive to the issues of addiction, so maybe that was the right thing. Paulie actually started when he was twelve because he hung out with the older kids in our neighborhood. He said he smoked his first cigarette when he was ten years old. He may have gotten on the wrong path pretty young. So maybe it was appropriate."

Most of the time my wife was the disciplinarian for the little things. But for something big, I played the bad guy. Like when Paulie got caught smoking. I hit him with the paddle once, not something I'm particularly proud of—nor something I'm ashamed of.

"I remember Danny and I were listening by the door," Cristin recalled. "I mean he hit him good. After that, the paddle hardly came out. I remember once my mom hit me with it so light, my brothers made fun of me for weeks."

When Paulie and I began working together building motorcycles, Cristin was apprehensive about our partnership. She wasn't crazy about the arrangement because at the time, Paulie was well established at the Ironworks. Plus, he'd gone back to attending church. I knew Cristin and her mother were concerned.

"I let Paulie know I was skeptical and scared about them going into this together. I guess I was very protective of Paulie, and at the time, he was doing well at the Ironworks. Our whole family—well, most of us—are Christians. And he had started going back to church and rededicated his life to God. That was very important to me, so I wanted him to stay on the good path. But I knew that their working relationship wasn't great. Working together makes it difficult to separate the personal from the business. It's impossible, actually. So I was concerned for both of them, that it could ruin their relationship."

I think after hearing the stories about my wild days and watching me go through the recovery process, Cristin has pretty much forsaken booze. There may have been a time around Paula's and my divorce when she was tempted to act out, but the counseling and the learning from my mistakes, as well as a good relationship with her mom, kept her on the straight and narrow. Drinking has never been her thing, and it still isn't.

"When I did drink, I didn't feel good. It felt empty to me pretty quickly, so I came to my own faith in God and decided I didn't want to do that stuff. I'll go out to bars with my friends and they'll drink, but I don't."

As with the rest of the Teutul family, the television show has had a tremendous impact. Cristin was away at college when the first pilot episode aired. Her response was typically Teutul: horror, then eventual acceptance.

"I watched it with my friends from college. I only told a few people, my roommate and a couple of my close friends. We didn't have cable in our room. We had to go to a lounge TV. We almost didn't find a TV.

"I didn't know what to expect. More like a documentary and not so much fighting. I wasn't that happy. I was disappointed. I wasn't ashamed. I've never felt ashamed of my family, ever. I felt more protective toward them. I didn't want them to be exposed, and that's what upset me. I didn't feel it was 100 percent honest or true. Even if they didn't mind the arguing, I minded.

"That's why I'm not a big fan of the show. I'll watch it sometimes to support them. But it's not my favorite thing in the world. I know that what they're doing actually happens, I don't deny any of that, although I think some of it is played up when they do the voice-overs."

Like it or not, the attention that the show has brought to my family has had its obvious advantages and disadvantages. The advantages are easy. Money. Creature comforts. The disadvantages. Fame. Public scrutiny. Family friction. Loss of privacy. Even Cristin, who chooses to remain away from the cameras, sometimes feels the collateral damage.

"In some ways, I'm sorry this thing has exploded. It brings a lot of problems. But I've benefited from it, too. My college is paid for. It's been a blessing not to have to worry about certain financial things that everyone else has to worry about. But there's a certain simplicity that's been taken away, and I miss that. I know I'm contradicting myself because everyone likes the comforts that having money brings. Nobody would say no to that. But other things come with it that I wish weren't there."

While most of the show's attention has been drawn to Paulie and my relationship, I'm sure it hasn't been 100 percent smooth between Cristin and her mother. Cristin chose to attend college and nursing school over working in the family business. Believe it or not, there are similarities between Paulie and my relationship and Cristin and her mother's. Fortunately, there are differences as well.

"We have the same intensity in that we love each other very much. What's different is, unlike working together like Paulie and my dad, I chose college and independence, and that's been healthy for our relationship. That's the difference. My dad and Paulie have stayed on top of each other. It's difficult to change things or work on things when you're right on top of each other. Not that it's impossible."

The question I like to ask is: If Cristin and her mom were in business together, and a camera crew followed *them* all day long, would it be any different than it is between Paulie, Mikey, and me?

"If my mother and I were on television like my father and brothers are, it would be different. Women think too much, while men don't think enough. I don't think my father and brother yell about the real issues. They just yell about what's going on at the time. My mother and I would be talking about the real issues. There would definitely be fighting and some intensity. There might be as much yelling, because that's my family. We yell about almost everything, which is something I'm trying to work on. But our battles would be more about counseling, therapy, and talking through it."

CHAPTER 18

Cameraman Steve Purcell stands still as Senior and Paulie prepare to split past him on their Military Auction Bikes. (Photo: Martin GM Kelly)

GONE RIDIN' OUT WEST

SENIOR:

Most of my early days of riding were short jaunts. I didn't do any long-distance cross-country runs. Just before I turned sober, I started hanging out a lot with a bike rider named Harry McLaughlin. Harry was a local Orange County guy who had done construction all his life. He also ran a karate school and was the baddest guy on two legs. He stood five-foot-seven, bad to the bone. He could walk into a bar and without exaggeration take on five guys at a time if he had to.

Harry and I were the same age, and we both rode Harleys and loved to raise hell together. No matter what the circumstances, if I had a problem, I could call Harry and he'd be there. He was a man who lived by his word. The real deal.

When we rode our bikes, we would go out for the whole day into the hinterlands beyond Orange and Ulster Counties. He led and I followed. When I rode with Harry, I never knew where the hell we were going. I just opened up the throttle and kept pace. If he'd ditched me and left me on my own, you might never have seen me again. Desolation added to the adventure of the ride. We would roar our way into the mountains, out past the reservoirs. The next thing I knew, the day was over. Harry and I would log in two or three hundred miles at a clip, and that was normal riding. I went from going on short hops to enjoying what riding was about. Expanded horizons. Now, not only did I enjoy building bikes and the way they looked and functioned, but I was a long-distance rider, too. Before I knew Harry, I'd barely left the state. Now single, sober, unattached, and on my own, I was riding free. Riding long distances helped me forget about alcohol. I felt more centered as a human being with the wind in my face. I had time to reflect on my life and dreams.

I first rode out west in 1998, across the Midwest then northwest toward Wyoming to the farthest end of Montana and back. It was the greatest feeling. Being a die-hard East Coast guy, I expected to go out west and be ambushed by black bears, snakes, and wild Indians. When I motored along the Beartooth Highway, on the border between Wyoming and Montana, I thought I'd died and gone to heaven. I saw many kinds of wildlife. I was closer to nature. The air was brisk and clean. It was a raw, revealing experience. Although the main Beartooth Highway is now closed, it's been aptly described as "the most beautiful highway in America." I was way up in the elevated wilderness loaded with mule deer, moose, and mountain goats; grizzly bears hunted for trout by the lakes and waterfalls. The nicest ride in the USA. Once you got to the top of the mountains, you were actually in the clouds. Lush forests and alpine air. When I pulled over and looked down from the top of the mountain, the road I'd just traveled looked like a shoestring.

When I'm riding my motorcycle, it's both an internal and external experience. I zone out to the outrageous scenery. I'm in tune with the rumble of the bike and the glide of the ride and the wind in my face. I like to listen to XM radio— '60s oldies and classic rock—and just let my mind wander. I might ponder building a new bike or being at home, sprawled on the couch with my girlfriend and my dogs Gus and Marty. I am wherever I want to be to the rhythm and the rumbling torque of a Harley touring bike.

My favorite ride out west is through Idaho, Montana, and Wyoming. And when I say *west,* I mean in the Rocky Mountains. I enter through Yellowstone National Park in Wyoming and come out in Montana. Then when I hit Montana, I move on to Virginia City and head up toward Glacier National Park. A motorcycle gives you the closest thing to what it might have been like riding the trails of the Wild West. I love the sensation of riding into Virginia City. It's an authentic Wild West town, frozen in time, just like the Gold Rush days of the 1800s. It's shades of the outlaw Old West. You pull your bike up to a hitching post and amble into an old saloon. You can smell that unforgettable scent of the brass taps. You feel like a cowboy. Free to ramble.

When I'm out west, I ride for the whole day. Up in the morning, I have an early breakfast, then we'll keep on rolling until we stop for dinner. My girlfriend and I ride

Harleys together through the national parks. To me, it's the ultimate thing in life. Ask me where on the planet I want to go when I have a week or two off. Forget Aruba, Club Med, or sitting on the beach; you can have those. I'm in a Wyoming state of mind. Give me a motorcycle and several hundred miles of open country road under a crisp, clear blue sky.

Paulie and Mike aren't the long-distance, rain-or-shine riders that I am. We rented bikes in Ireland, Scotland, and England when we filmed a few episodes in Europe. We went out together on a daylong run through the Irish countryside. We rode the Ring of Kerry in Ireland, which was a hellish five-hour ride around a mountain of the worst roads you've ever seen in your life. Beautiful scenery, but unfortunately only the last 1 percent of the ride was gorgeous. Rolling hills. We did the ride for one of the episodes. They used about ten seconds of it.

I remember it as a long winding trip, my arms and back surprisingly hurting when we got back. And we rode through Scotland. We putted around Edinburgh on rented scooters wearing kilts with the wind blowing up my crotch, learning to ride on the wrong side of the road and mastering the roundabouts, which the Brits have instead of four-way intersections. It was the closest thing to being out west with its lush greenery and zigzag roads, dotted with pleasant small villages and timeless castle ruins.

I've ridden to California only a few times, but what I'd like to do one day is to ride south all the way down on Highway 1's two-lane coastal stretch along the Pacific Ocean. I'd start up at the northern end in Half Moon Bay and scoot straight down past San Simeon and Pismo Beach into Santa Barbara (a surf dog city where Mikey likes to hang out); roll on through to Malibu on the PCH (Pacific Coast Highway), roaring past Long Beach and San Diego; and then roll on down to TJ and deeper into Mexico. What sucks about riding in California, though, is the traffic. When I'm on two wheels, I don't want cars lined up for miles.

Come to think of it, New York State isn't so different from being out west. You can get on your bike and ride forever; head out for a couple of hours, and you're way off into the boondocks. Small towns. Farmlands. Currier & Ives scenery. No traffic. Beautiful forests. So many people mistakenly think of New York as one big city.

I get a 360-degree panoramic view when I ride because I like to wear a light helmet that sits on the top of my head. People ask me how I feel about helmet laws. Personally, I don't like 'em. I'd rather have the *option* of wearing one or not. If you feel insecure, then go ahead and put one on. It's okay when it's cold outside, but when it's ninety degrees and humid, you don't want to be riding with a bucket on your head.

I believe that a full DOT-approved helmet deters your ability to ride safely. It kills the fun. Helmets can mess with your peripheral vision. They can restrict your sight lines.

Like a lot of our fans, celebrities who love to ride bikes stop by to visit the shop. All kinds of actors, musicians, and artists are fans of the show, and they often pop by (sometimes unannounced) for a personal tour. Once Nicolas Cage stopped by and we gave him a tour. Then one of my favorite actors, Armand Assante, stopped by and introduced himself. One of the most memorable visits was when actor Ewan McGregor, Charley Boorman, and their film crew finished up their round-the-world motorcycle trip and rode into Orange County. Ewan had been by previously and talked to Paulie and our general manager Steve Moreau about planning their round-the-world run on BMWs.

Ewan McGregor is the real deal. He lives what he does. He's respectful, and he even looks up to me. I think he's seen every episode of our show. He likes to talk bikes. A real motorhead. A guy you want to be around, a for-real guy. That he traveled around the world on a motorcycle tells you something about what an interesting guy he is. It had to be one rough ride, but they loved it. They stopped at OCC headquarters on the next-to-the-last leg of their worldwide journey. Paulie, Mikey, and I with a pack of shop guys rode in with Ewan and Charley as they filmed their documentary. We were thrilled to ride into Manhattan with those guys, going over the George Washington Bridge together. It was a highlight for us.

During one of my special trips out west, I brought along Steven Tyler, the lead singer of Aerosmith. We were on a plane together the first time I met him. Then we did a charity event in Daytona, and that's where we first hung out and became friends. Harley-Davidson rounded up a couple of bikes for us and we rode out from Fort Lauderdale to St. Augustine, a pretty cool ride. We hit it off right away, mostly because we're both from Yonkers. We grew up five miles apart. Steve is very eccentric, an authentic rock star. He's got so much going on in his head; he bounces around the walls when you're with him. Like me, he's lived the crazy life. Been and seen it all. What I respect about Steve is that he's now a grounded guy who values his family and his kids. Like *American Chopper,* Aerosmith appeals to a fan base ranging from nine to ninety.

During the summer of 2005, I phoned Steven and woke him up out of bed at six thirty in the morning to tell him he was going out riding with me. I had planned a fifteen-hundred-mile trip from the Grand Canyon all the way to Glacier National Park in Montana. I sent a plane to pick Steven up, and we rode through Montana and Wyoming, stopping off in Yellowstone Park and Virginia City. I think he had a good time, although he couldn't finish the entire trip because he needed to be in Hawaii. We spent seven hours a day cruising on two-thousand-pound Screaming Eagle touring bikes. I pushed Steve pretty hard the whole way, just like Harry McLaughlin did to me years earlier, and we topped off at speeds of up to 120 miles per hour. Steven hung in there like a champ and rode four days with me, dropping the bike four times. The last time he dropped the bike, I took a picture of us with the bike on the ground and my hands strangling his neck.

We were rolling. There was no time for heavy partying. By the end of each day, we barely had enough energy to get through dinner. I can only imagine what people thought when we walked into diners and filling stations. We were recognized everywhere on the road. After we'd make it through one town, by the time we got to the next, people had called ahead to their friends. Everybody knew we were coming.

That happens a lot. One time I was riding through Florida outside Daytona with my girlfriend when her motorcycle broke down behind me. By the time I realized she was stuck on the roadside and I was able to get back around to her and the bike, a crowd of people had already pulled off the highway and were waving and running toward me, asking for photo ops and autographs. I wanted to take care of my girlfriend's broken-down bike. It turned into a roadside personal appearance.

Whenever we're in Southern California, we love to stop by and visit Jay Leno. Jay's the real deal, too. We like going out to dinner and hanging out with him. He *loves* his car collection. His cars are like his family. He'll take you through the entire collection, and he knows absolutely everything about every automobile he owns. Jay isn't just some rich guy who buys cars because they look nice. He knows every little weird detail about each car.

After we were on the *Tonight Show,* Jay Leno commissioned us to build him a bike. He matched us up with one of his favorite vintage bikes from the 1920s. The custom Jay Leno Bike we built was awesome. It was a throwback to an old Brough Superior, the same bike that T. E. Lawrence of *Lawrence of Arabia* fame made notorious by killing himself on one. Our creation looked like an older ride, only it had a rake and stretch. Jay loves that bike and rides it anytime we come down. While we were building his bike, we kept him in the dark about it, and I think he was getting a little aggravated with us. But when we unveiled it on the show, we brought along our crew to film us doing the *Tonight Show* presenting him with his bike. It made for great TV.

Jay's a cool guy. He calls up and likes to chat about bikes. One time he phoned up Paulie at the shop. "Hey, Paul, it's Jay Leno," he said, doing his unmistakable shtick. "What's going on? I just got the cologne. Now I smell like a Teutul."

David Letterman is also one of our biggest fans. He rides a Harley. Like Jay, Letterman is a motorhead. He owns his own Indy car team and loves to watch our show. Our exchanges with him on the show are very New York, even though he's from Indiana. We bust butt back and forth, and Letterman is no kiss-ass. If he doesn't like you, you'll know. We once heard that David talked about us so much one time on the *Late Show* that the brass at CBS called him about plugging the Discovery Channel too much.

When we appeared on *The Daily Show with Jon Stewart* on Comedy Central, we found out that he and his wife are big *American Chopper* fans, too. When we arrived on the set, Jon's wife had come down to the studio to meet us. She was as excited to meet us as we were to be on Jon's show.

People often ask me if OCC choppers are practical bikes to ride, or if they're difficult. There will always be people out there who will say choppers aren't practical rides, but most of the bikers who say that are the same people who haven't ridden one. There's a certain mind-set and attitude that comes with riding choppers. Look at it this way: Why do you wear a three-piece suit to work? Why not wear jogging pants and a sweatshirt instead? They're much more comfortable and practical. You can run faster in them. Why would you wear a suit? Well, it's the same principle getting on a chopper. It's supercool. It's different. It's dressy. It has its own unique feeling and dynamic, as opposed to just getting on a Yamaha or a Suzuki and zooming off.

How come choppers have made such a huge comeback? Maybe it's because they never went away. Choppers are like rock and roll. No matter how you look at them, they're just plain cool. With an OCC chopper, you don't hear people say, *Oh man, that's just a chopper. Those are so yesterday.* Choppers are always going to be the symbol of American hell-raising ingenuity. Again, it's like rock and roll. If you're an American, rock and roll and choppers are forever. Choppers might never go out of style. But if they do, they'll slip away for a couple of years then come roaring back.

Another issue is Old School versus New School, which is something Paulie and I deal with at the shop daily. Our designer, Jason "Pohly" Pohl, defined it this way: "In terms of modern chopper design, OCC New School design is a more modern, sleek look that's both cool and new age. It forces people to look. The criticism of New School choppers might be that they're difficult to handle or that they're too fancy. And who has time to clean up that chrome?

"Old School is determined by the suspension setup of the bike," Jason continued. "It's rigid in the back with a spring or a Leaf Springer on the front end.

ORANGE COUNTY CHOPPERS

The Orange Bobber, with its off-the-hook front wheel, is one of Senior's finest Old School designs. (Photo: OCC Archives)

Sometimes we can combine the two genres. For instance, our Cherokee Casino Bike has an Old School front end put on a modern bike. So you *can* mix the two. Handlebars are sometimes a giveaway. If they're ape hangers, it's Old School. The biggest giveaway of an Old School style is the rake and the front tire. If the front tire is not pushed out away from the bike a good distance, then it's an Old School design. Old School is an easier bike to ride. A criticism of Old School bikes is that they can be dorky and ride rough."

Same difference with choppers versus Japanese bikes. Yeah, they're fast, but they're made out of plastic! They're going to be quicker off the line. They have great engineering. The Japanese build nice bikes, but it's like the difference between driving a Honda Civic and a 1969 Chevy Camaro. A Camaro is heavy and muscular. Sheer power, brute strength, muscle car, and American-made. Chromed steel and aluminum

T6061. Not plastic. When I'm rolling through the mountains or the back roads of Orange County, I have no need to go two hundred mph. The high whining sound of a Japanese bike's got nothing on the deep ballsy rumble of a chopper. You can't compare the two, other than the fact that they both have two wheels.

And finally, we don't bad-mouth Harley-Davidson motorcycles. We think Harley-Davidson is a great company. These bikes are American-made, and they'll continue to set the trend for many generations to come. Compared with the bikes we build—well, Harleys and OCC choppers are apples and oranges. The rake, the style, and the factory look of a Harley are so much different from what I love about our choppers. With Harleys, the contour of the bike doesn't flow as much as I prefer. It doesn't look as sculpted. It's the difference between a bike that rolls off an assembly-line floor and a one-of-a-kind customized design. But still, all bike riders can remember their first Harley like they can remember the first love of their life. What more can I say?

19

Fabricator Rick Petko dons eye protection and a mellow disposition at OCC. (Photo: Martin GM Kelly)

RICK PETKO: MASTER FABRICATOR

RICK:

I started working at OCC on July 21, 2003, and it was a whole lot different then than it is now. Smaller shop. Not as high profile.

It started as a fluke. I'd heard of the shop mostly through the work that Senior and Junior were doing as builders. One day I was on my way up to Laconia Bike Week, riding up Highway 84 from Pennsylvania, when I noticed the exit nearest to the Orange County Choppers shop. It wasn't that far out of my way, so on the ride back I called them up out of the blue. The first guy I talked to was Steve Moreau, OCC's general manager. He invited me to come on down.

I'm from the Nazareth area of Pennsylvania. I live right by the racetrack. Like a lot of folks, I'd seen *American Chopper* on television. At the time, they had shot only a handful of episodes. They'd just started the first season and had finished filming Mikey's Blues Bike. In fact, they were doing the filming for it when I stopped by the shop. That was when they were on Stone Castle Road off Route 17K in an industrial park, about six miles down the road from the current Factory Street location. The bike shop was in the same general location as the Ironworks. It was a small place. They had just moved from the downstairs to the upstairs.

When I first talked to Senior and Junior at OCC, I could tell they needed a fabricator to help out Vinnie DiMartino. Paulie needed someone who could do everything and help him out, too. Prior to the time I joined, I was doing auto restorations. Before that, I did big industrial steel contracting work for ten years. I worked with large steel, plate steel, and beams. I worked in cement companies and steel foundries. Mostly big industry. It was nothing like what Senior had going at the Ironworks, doing railings and stairways. But I've always worked on motorcycles, and I've owned and ridden bikes ever since I could walk.

In the steel business, I'd travel up and down the East Coast working at different kinds of plants. But that was getting old quick. After ten years of it, I couldn't take it anymore, and I quit. I started my own business for a while, doing decks and fences. I also had a pressure-washing, sealing, and staining business. I was doing auto restorations. But I've always had a passion for working on bikes. At the time I talked to OCC, my cousin and I were working on getting the equipment together to have a shop and do bike restorations. I guess that's what attracted me to get off the freeway and go visit OCC in the first place. My love of bikes.

I consider myself primarily a fabricator. A fabricator is someone who makes stuff out of raw steel. It could be sheet metal. Round bar or angles. A fabricator builds stuff from scratch. And a good fabricator can fabricate anything out of anything. Handlebars out of steel bars. Fenders out of sheet metal. That sort of thing.

Here at OCC, I don't have a job title per se. Fabricator, I guess. Other than that, who knows? We do so much. When I got the job, I wanted to get back to working closely with bikes, and at a higher level than what I'd been doing in the past. And I've achieved that. Honestly, it was that simple. A shot in the dark. I knew there were a lot of people applying at OCC at the time, putting in their applications, but my coming in was a freak thing. I didn't know anybody who knew anyone. I just came in cold.

When I first met with Senior and Junior, I immediately sensed they needed a jack-of-all-trades on their team. Someone willing to learn and stretch out. I told them I'd made gas tanks before, and that *really* sparked their interest. I was honest in telling them what I liked to do and what I could do. I didn't BS them, and I guess they believed me because they didn't check on any of my references. Both Junior and Senior practically hired me on the spot.

It felt good to be hired out of trust and instinct. The early OCC was like that then. Still, a lot of people ask me, "How *did* you start working with them?" When I started working there, I didn't have much interest in the television show. I was way more interested in the quality of their custom bike builds. I was a good fit because I loved building bikes. To be honest, the show was irrelevant to me in a way. Before they officially hired me, Senior asked me if I was camera-shy, like it was some joke. But it was no joke. My job turned into doing stuff for the show, on camera.

When I was first hired, my job was to do the service work on the customer bikes and fabricate. But then my responsibilities expanded beyond repairs into fabricating. I'd be downstairs, and then I'd run upstairs. Then downstairs again, running back and forth doing various service and fabrication duties.

In the beginning, I was nervous about working on TV. Plus, it was weird having cameras hovering around. At first, it slowed down my productivity a little. But I didn't have it so bad. It was a lot tougher on Ronnie Salsbury, our operations manager. He's the guy under the gun. It's his job to see to it that the bikes—whether they're TV bikes or custom orders—get built and out the door on time.

Besides the bikes we build on TV, we actually have a lot of other theme bikes and individual customer bikes that are built off camera that are also under contract and deadline. Vinnie and I have to hustle to get those done on time, too. And sometimes the filming holds up that process. Nowadays they hire on more guys, which helps; before that, poor Vinnie had to build those bikes in between doing the on-camera projects. There were breaks here and there when Vinnie and I would have to hurry up and try to get as much done on the side as we could so we could go back to filming. Switching back and forth like that definitely slows things down.

Some of the bikes we build are designed for riding, while others are built for pure show. It depends on the customer. Or the company. I don't show any favoritism for bikes that are built on camera versus the custom bikes created off camera. As far as I'm concerned, the same passion and effort go into both. Whatever bike it's going to be, whether it's built on TV or not, a camera can't change how good it's going to turn out. So I stay focused. I get into a mind-set and I'll know exactly what I'm doing and what needs to get done and when. Normally, I like to tune out everything around me, get into what I'm doing and just do it. But when the cameras are in your face, sometimes you have to stop and redo things to make sure the camera sees what you're doing. Or sometimes I'll have to flip around and do the same thing on the other side for a different camera angle. Now, that gets weird sometimes.

By now, everybody at OCC is accustomed to the cameras. But back in the beginning, it affected things a lot more. When I first started here, Vinnie was twelve bikes behind in his regular mock-ups! So when I started, Vinnie and I hammered those bikes out as quickly as possible. Since Junior can't do as much with the off-TV bikes, Jason Pohl more or less handles the designing on those.

A lot of times, Jason will talk with the customer to see what bike they want.

Then they'll hammer it out together and draw it up. Sometimes they won't know exactly what it takes for a guy like me to build something. Something may look cool on paper, but in reality, it might be difficult or impractical to build. So we'll make the necessary adjustments. Jason does a great job getting it right the first time.

It's difficult to put a label on Junior's OCC design style. I'd say he's more of a new age stylist, but then again he likes the older stuff, too. While he can design an older-style bike, I think it's his preference to go modern.

I like working with both Junior and Senior. Junior's work is more contemporary, and he's good to work with. He's open to suggestions about anything, and not once since I've worked here has he said, "This is my way and this is how I want it done because this is my company." He doesn't act in that manner, which is surprising. You'd think it would happen sometime. But it hasn't. Both Junior and Senior have entirely different tastes and styles, and that's what makes working here fun. Senior and I enjoy the same style of bikes. We share a lot of the same tastes in classic motorcycles.

Rick on the job, grinding and blending.
(Photo: Martin GM Kelly)

As far as personal tastes go, I guess I'm more of an Old School bike guy. I like more of the Old School choppers from the 1960s and the '70s, catering to the Old School parts instead of creating everything from machines and computers, although I can do both. You can make a lot of cool stuff on machines and computers, especially for the TV theme bikes, like everything on the Snap-on Tool Bike. I also did a lot of work on the Sam's Club Bike and the Discovery Bike featuring those crazy dinosaur/reptile parts, like fins sticking up on the fenders. The theme bikes are pretty wild, but one of my favorite jobs was building Paul Senior's Old School collection. Old School is more my way, with the look, better cornering, and a lower center of gravity.

One of the bikes, an orange one that we call the Bobber, was built in ten days. I made the gas tank in a 1920s style. Half the tank was for gas, the other half for oil. We built it for the Journey Museum in Sturgis. Another orange bike, the Orange Knuckle, was the second bike Senior and I did together in the series. It's a rigid-frame chopper, which is more my style than the modern Softail bikes that have a softer ride with rear suspension. Paul Senior's Corvette Bike is my style. Since I joined OCC, I've worked on just about every bike done on TV, except for a handful. Modern or Old School, Hardtail or Softail, I can build them all. My résumé or body of work seems to be growing steadily. I had posters made up of the bikes that I've worked on and so far I've accumulated a helluva collection.

People ask me how accurate *American Chopper* is in showing an average day on the job at OCC. Often the TV show will accurately portray the true dynamics of what it's like to work there. Then sometimes it's way off. Since they're shooting hundreds of hours of footage to jam into a one-hour episode, I guess there's bound to be some distortion. But they're right on the money. A lot of people ask me, Do Senior and Junior really fight like that? I say, Yeah, they sure do, and they'll argue at any given time. There are times when the cameras are shut off because of the fighting. And that's real. I would honestly say that nothing you see on the show is made up.

Senior and Junior both have their own issues from the past, that's for sure, with Senior being an alcoholic and everything. Maybe they've settled most of them, or else they have a lot more unresolved stuff they're trying to deal with. It's hard to say for sure. But either way, the conflict is an ongoing thing.

Nowadays the show deals with a lot more personalities in the shop, and it focuses in on real working people. That's what appeals to our viewers. They see us as people who aren't much different than they are. We get toothaches. We have doctor's appointments. People yell. We have accidents. We have kids. It's strange sometimes being a celebrity now. I sign autographs, and sometimes I'll go out alone for personal appearances—that's interesting. I was up in Boston one weekend by myself representing the show and the shop. People recognized me on the street. I'm just this guy who likes building bikes and welding, and now I'm a TV personality. Isn't it strange how people react to the power of television?

What's more amazing is the age range of people this show attracts. I can't get over that. I'll see kids at personal appearances who are three years old lined up with their parents. I'll have families come up to me with their daughters who are taking welding classes in high school. These girls are so proud and pumped up, and they stand in line just to tell me about it. One mother told me that her daughter had worked on a John Deere tractor, and the John Deere Company contacted them and wanted her to do something with them. According to her mom, I was an inspiration to her. It's hard to believe. All that from a TV show.

My biggest influence in the bike and hot rod world has to be my dad. He painted bikes when I was younger, so I started out painting bikes, too. I'd look through his magazines and, like Senior, check out the David Mann pictures and the cool metal choppers. That's where it started for me, with those David Mann paintings. And bikes by Arlen Ness. And cars by Big Daddy Roth.

One of the main perks of the job at OCC is getting to meet some of the legends. I once met George Barris, the guy who built so many of the famous classic show cars during the 1960s. I also met Chip Foose from the TV show *Overhaulin'*. And both of them knew me, which was a compliment! As far as bike builders go, I admire the work of Billy Lane and Jesse James. The late Indian Larry, another super Old School guy, has been very influential for me.

Before I came to OCC, I must admit, I'd never heard of a motorcycle being called a "theme bike." Now there are lots of people doing them. While OCC might have started the ball rolling, I would venture to say that every customized bike has some ongoing theme to its design, one way or another.

Sometimes for me, building a corporate bike can get a little over the top. I've been known to cringe. For instance, building a bike for PEZ? They're a cool company, and I love PEZ, but is there a bike there? That's weird. Even a company like Gillette. I think we had our doubts about that one, too. Razors and motorcycles? But then when the bikes come out looking great, it works out. In my opinion, sometimes the corporate thing takes away from the raw biker end of things, but then I'm the guy who prefers building those Old School choppers with Senior.

Me, I love to ride motorcycles. That's the bottom line. I would ride every day of the year if I could. I ride to work as often as I can, which is saying something because I commute ninety-five miles each way every day from Pennsylvania to New York. It's nice to take a break and get outside and ride with the guys at OCC. One of the coolest rides we took together was taking the POW/MIA Bike down to Washington, DC. We led the annual procession to the Wall for Memorial Day. That was a very moving experience for me, because not only is my relative's name on the Wall, but we also put it on the bike.

It's tough, but we ride as much as we can together at OCC. One ride we did was when they were filming us from a helicopter. It was supposed to be for a new beginning clip for the show, but they didn't use it. I remember the time we rode into New York together with Ewan McGregor and Charley Boorman for their TV show and book, *Long Way Round*. I'll always remember riding across the George Washington Bridge into Manhattan that day. It was the end of their long journey, and they were filming us from a helicopter, too. I remember going across the bridge and tearing it up in the pack. What a rush.

People often ask me the difference between the duties Vinnie and I perform at OCC. Probably the biggest difference between what Vinnie does and what I do is that he does a lot more of the electrical and wiring and exhausts than me, and I do more gas tanks. Other than that, our responsibilities are pretty much the same. We're both craftsmen and fabricators. Vinnie's good at stringing the electrical, while I don't care for it. Me, I'd much rather be hammering on a cool new tank design. And riding.

Senior and the kids. Left to right: Mikey, Paulie, Cristin, Danny, and Senior. (Photo: Paula Teutul personal collection)

DAN: GOING HIS OWN WAY IN THE STEEL BIZ

DANNY TEUTUL:

I'm the second son, born in 1977. I was the youngest child for a while, and then my brother Mikey and my sister, Cristin, came along. Right now I see myself not as on the outside, but as free. I get a few of the perks by hanging around. I can be at one of the bike shows and nobody will recognize me. I can still go out in public. I'm like the mysterious third Osbourne.

I've worked for my father since I was thirteen and then again out of high school. I worked hard for him. When I first started at the Ironworks, I couldn't even turn a nut. I didn't know anything about mechanics or construction. Then I started picking it up. I liked it because it was something new, and I kept getting better at it. Hard work was what brought me around. That and the will to learn. When I was working for my father, I tried to stay away from the *boss's-son* mentality. I was working Saturdays, Sundays, as much as I could.

I went out on my own at twenty-seven in 2004. Right now I own Orange County Ironworks. I can make my own decisions and come and go as I please. I have people who work for me, who I think respect me. At first we had some problems, and I caused a few with my inexperience. It was basically trial by fire. Once we started getting some work, though, we got our act together. We cut the fat here and there, hired some key people, moved some folks around, and got some systems in place. That's taken about two years.

My childhood wasn't too bad, and you hate to complain when so many people have had it much worse. So in a way it was pretty normal. We lived on a dead-end street with a lot of kids. We were always playing sports when I was in high school, whether it was basketball, football, or working out. I had bikes. Three or four bikes, but never a Harley. They were rice rockets, and I never felt really comfortable riding them. I was worried about hitting something on the highway.

As far as my home life goes, it really wasn't too bad. Looking back, I think my father could have given me more advice and guidance. But the big thing he did was get up and go to work every day. I don't remember much about my father's drinking. I was spared a lot of that. But sometimes they say you develop during your first couple of years, and that's what makes you who you are. So while I didn't see it, maybe it did affect me.

My parents fought, but I thought it was healthy for your parents to fight. At least they were talking. And while I found our family somewhat normal, looking back, I guess it was a little abnormal here and there.

I remember first seeing the TV show and thinking, *It's going to be huge.* I felt from the start that it was really going to take off. With all the fake reality stuff on TV, it was perfect timing, with the bikes and the family dysfunction. To me, they're my family. It's a weird situation, and I don't even know if it's totally hit how odd it is. I don't know if it ever will.

The show is real because I've seen them fight a million times in the steel shop. People ask me if they really fight like that. Yes. Is it staged? Maybe, but I would say that 98 percent of the time it's real. Paulie's a little laid-back, but I don't think he's that bad.

I run my shop differently. There's not much yelling. A lot of communication. It's a different management style. My father is more into snap decisions. We take a lot of risks, too, but I think as far as employees go, I try to offer a little more support. While my father was always in charge—and I learned a lot from that—when it was my turn to run a business, I didn't want to push too many people around.

I had a good time working with Mikey. I was always chasing him out of bed. These days, Mikey seems like he's in a good position. Happy. He doesn't need much. He wants for almost nothing. That's the way he's always been. He never needed money, so that's not been much of a motivation for him.

Before the TV show, it was tempting to join up when they first started the bike shop because they were always going out on the road to fun places like Daytona. I remember when I went to Biketoberfest and saw their first photo shoot with the coffin tank bike. I was there when the bike wouldn't start, and the headlight was falling off. That was my father's first photo shoot.

Regarding the freedom thing, if I wanted to push it, I guess I could have gone in with those guys and still come home and enjoyed my family. My kids are great. They're the centerpieces of the family right now.

Sometimes people see my last name, and suddenly we're best friends. Coming from a business where people knew my father, it's a constant struggle to separate myself. I'm overshadowed by OCC. People bring it up, and I try to handle it, but after a while I get tired of it. Still, I'm very proud of what they're doing at OCC. It took work. Were they in the right place at the right time? Yes, but they still had to be there in the first place. Then they had to keep things going. They were in the right place, and while the show on Discovery made them who they are, they made themselves bigger instead of just sitting in the garage like other people might have done, spending their money. Instead, they built up OCC.

As far as not being on the show goes, I do regret not going to the New York Jets training camp with them—I'm a huge Jets fan. Other than that, well, no, I don't have any regrets. I know where I stand with things. While I don't watch the show regularly, I'm happy that they are where they are. At the same time, I have a lot, too. My life is quieter, and sometimes I think they're the ones who should be jealous of me.

The cost of all this fame and fortune remains to be seen. I know they *like* the fame, but I don't know how much they *enjoy* it. They travel all the time, and they have a lot of good experiences, but there are safety and security issues. You have to watch your public persona. You have to be careful.

My father and brother Paulie's relationship has always been the same, but it's not such a dramatic thing for me. Sure, they're going to fight and they're going to be father and son forever. Hopefully their relationship will get a little healthier with some communication here and there. My father is a good person. I just had issues sometimes with his management style, that's all.

Senior and his bull mastiff Gus relax in his OCC office. BTW, Senior's on the left. (Photo: Martin GM Kelly)

THE MAN BEHIND THE MUSTACHE

MIKE:

I once wrote a tribute to my father for *V-Twin* magazine. I mentioned in the article how sometimes people come up to me and call my father names. This bothers me. What kind of person would do such a thing? People who don't really know him.

My dad is a man of little or no pretense. While he likes his bad-ass persona and doesn't hesitate to let anybody know how he feels about certain things, the most popular misconception about him is that he freaks out all the time. Over the slightest thing. On the contrary. He's mellowed over time. Yes, he yells periodically, and of course he and my brother rub each other the wrong way, so there's friction there. But even when my dad's super pissed off at me, he doesn't really freak out that much.

My dad took a major risk starting up Orange County Choppers. It was during the period in a dad's life when most fathers might have stayed put in a job they hated and remained miserable. Not my dad. He did something remarkable. He started a business building things he really loves. Choppers. He followed his dreams. And that takes courage. He could have retired and sat pretty, but you've got to admire a guy who takes his life nut, cashes it in on some chips, and then puts it all on the red. I'm happy that he saved me from having to stay in the Ironworks business. I owe it all to him.

A lot of people see my father as bullheaded and stubborn. He readily admits to both traits. But over time, my father has relented on his neurotic pursuit of perfection. He now lets a lot more stuff slide, and with the growth of OCC, he's been forced to trust people more. And he's adapted to the challenge of trust, which is one of the hardest things a man can do, especially someone as stubborn as my dad. It must have been really hard for him to adjust to so many changes at fifty-three, the age he was when he and Paulie first started the chopper business. The progress my father has made over the past decade astounds me. If you were to tell me ten years ago that Paul Teutul would have changed so radically—starting a business, mellowing out, trusting people—I would never have believed it.

When you work with someone like my father, in order to succeed in the company, you have to be prepared to deal with a demanding personality. I get away with murder because he and I don't conflict so much. My other brothers butt heads, and that's okay. But once two stubborn people get into a yelling match, you're probably not going to get anywhere. You're stuck. So I don't even go there. And it's not that I spinelessly back down. I just think there's an art to dealing with my father that matches my disposition. Being patient and easygoing.

My father is an easy read, a straightforward guy to figure out. He likes things consistent. He loves reliability. He likes it when people are punctual. He admires people who are assertive. He prefers a person with a sense of humor who can take a joke and has thick skin. People who don't take crap from anybody. Anybody with any of those character traits will go a long way with my father.

In a sense, my dad is a loner. He doesn't hang out much with people. He loves his dogs. Loves being with his girlfriend. He loves peace and quiet away from the shop. Unless he's traveling on business, he doesn't really go out that much.

Unlike most TV celebrities, recognition in public isn't a problem with my dad. While he doesn't like being grabbed at—who does?—he actually likes it when people come up to him. He's like a kid about fame. He doesn't mind being recognized. Being famous is exciting to him, as opposed to being some kind of ego boost. When he's eating out, for instance, I've seen him get up in the middle of his meal and take pictures with fans. Personally, I can't handle that. That's above and beyond the call. But with my dad, it's as if being recognized is still something new, as if he hasn't gotten used to it.

My father has brought a great presence to the motorcycle business. Power and an intimidating strength. That's mainly because of his physical appearance. But he also has an inexplicable aura of leadership. People listen to him. Then they choose to follow him.

ORANGE COUNTY CHOPPERS

Rick and Senior apply the finishing touches to
the Vintage Bike. (Photo: Martin GM Kelly)

Many of the younger employees around the shop are frightened of him at first. Then once they get to know him, they respect him. They know that if they do a good job and put in an honest day's work, he'll take care of them. His true role in the company is hard to explain. He's in charge at OCC, but he delegates responsibility and has people under him who he listens to before major decisions are made. No question, if he weren't in charge, nothing here would run as smoothly.

Contrary to what you might see on the tube, I honestly don't think my dad carries a lot of anger. I know he's had anger issues in the past, but through counseling and 12-step programs, he's learned to lay a lot of his anger down and put it aside. Like I said, there's an art to dealing with him. Sometimes if you grant him one point, he'll relent on the remaining issues to compromise for the greater good. He now sees the broader picture. Dealing with my dad is all about explaining things to him. Talking to him and making common sense. He now knows that even if he's pissed off at something or somebody, in the overall scheme of things, sometimes it's best to let go, which is amazing, especially for someone as stubborn as my dad.

My dad's a simple guy. It's easy to make him happy. Both professionally and personally. I don't even think the big house on the hill matters all that much, because he only sits in his one favorite chair. He enjoys material possessions like his car collection. But if he didn't have them tomorrow, I honestly don't think he'd be that concerned. If he had to choose, he cares more about his dogs than his cars. If I wrecked one of his cars, as long as we had a good time doing it, I don't think he'd have any qualms. For instance, we've wrecked a lot of stuff at the shop. When we moved out of our old shop, we crashed a truck right through the office walls. I think he'd give up almost anything for a good laugh.

In recent years, my dad has become an adventuresome spirit, more so than I would have ever predicted. When the rest of us get vacation time, we lie on the beach. Not my dad. He'll go out and hit some hard highways up in the mountains. He loves it, and he's doing more and more riding. Just the fact that he would take a week away from work, cut himself off from everybody, and go out riding is a major stretch from the workaholic I used to know.

He loves working out. It's a release for him. He actually enjoys pumping iron and exercise, while most of us do it out of guilt and necessity. For my dad, working out has been a steady recreational activity for over twenty years. He's not one of those guys who hangs out and socializes at the gym and stares at his arms in the mirror. If he wanted to be some sort of muscle-bound facade, he'd probably be taking steroids. On the contrary. He'll go in, pump his iron, and leave. In fact, these days he does most of his workouts at the shop.

I guess the number one thing I love about my father is that no matter what happens, he's always there. He'll never turn his back on us. We love his ability to laugh at himself. He's well aware of his faults. But at this point in his life, he's a done deal. No excuses, just honesty. My dad is a meat-and-potatoes kind of guy. He likes a good steak and it better be cooked right. Or else he'll definitely let you know about it.

When it comes to my father, I don't harbor any aggression. It's the way I'm wired. I let stuff slide. Sometimes, though, he gets a bad rap as a hothead. And while everybody's entitled to certain feelings about him, I just wanted to set the record straight and write about his other side.

Sparks fly as Mike Ammirati grinds the frame on an OCC production bike. (Photo: Martin GM Kelly)

BUILDING THE PERFECT BEAST; OR, SO YOU WANNA OWN AN OCC CHOPPER?

SENIOR:

Every week, the television world watches the process of Orange County Choppers building custom bikes. But what's the process *behind the process* of building a chopper? Do you have to be a big corporation to own an Orange County Chopper? Can anyone order one? Are they affordable for the average rider? Even if you're not in the market, maybe you're simply curious about what goes on behind the scenes, from start to finish, as a custom OCC motorcycle progresses from a phone inquiry to the hands of a happy, excited customer.

Within a year's time, Orange County Choppers went from six employees to sixty. We now have a large building on Factory Street in Montgomery off Route 17K. We're the dominant industry in the Montgomery-Newburgh area. The speed at which this company grew was mind blowing. Yet with the television show, the merchandising, the personal appearances, and the licensing deals, building custom choppers is still OCC's primary concern. And at the core of our organization is an army of guys and gals whose job is to get bikes from the ordering phase to the riding stage as quickly as possible. Remember, we build a custom product, handmade to specification. We're not into cranking out bikes like sausages. So here's a behind-the-scenes glimpse of what we go through in building the perfect beast.

Ultimately, the responsibility for building an OCC chopper falls directly onto the shoulders of our director of operations, Ron Salsbury. In the beginning, just after Paulie and I emerged from our basement, wrenches and torches in hand, we formed Orange County Choppers, headquartered in a fifty-by-fifty-foot corner of our Orange County Ironworks. During those early days, I remember Ron sitting at a desk and answering the phone, taking orders for a T-shirt, then for a front end, then, if it was a good day, a bike order. There was very little organization to speak of. But that changed after the first and second television pilots aired, when we were catapulted from a small father-and-son business to having to build a company from the ground up.

Our early staff grew to include Paulie, one secretary, Ron, Vinnie DiMartino, Christian Welter, Cody Connelly, Nick Hansford, me, and then Mikey. By then, though, the business was spinning out of control. The phones were ringing off the hook. It was nuts.

Ron and the Teutul family go way back. Ron and Paulie grew up together through high school. Ron was also a weight-lifting buddy. Ron worked at my steel shop for nine years before he took off for the Big Apple. After 9/11, like a lot of city folks, he returned to his native Hudson Valley, just after the first show aired. We were swamped at the time and desperately needed someone to organize our company. Ron accepted the job, or—should I say—the ultimate challenge.

It didn't take long for Ron to realize he was in way over his head. Each month, the company was getting bigger. He recommended Steve Moreau, a longtime friend also from the Orange County area, who was intrigued enough to leave the two businesses he was running to come over and set up a brand-new corporate structure as OCC's general manager. Like a lot of OCC employees, what Steve lacked in formal corporate experience he more than made up for in balls and brains. He's been at the helm of our company ever since, everything from laying down phone lines, moving around desks, and putting up offices to evaluating and hiring staff and cutting large corporate deals. You can find Steve in the mornings before work jamming on his Les Paul guitar with the other OCC rivetheads inside the tiny boiler room. To say that Steve is important to our organization is an understatement. He and Ron experienced firsthand our explosive growth and have weathered the stress and pressures it took to put OCC on the fast track.

Back to the bikes, though. Ron still oversees the everyday operations of our shop. He's solely responsible for the production bikes OCC builds. He's in charge of the employees working in the shop. The OCC pecking order now goes approximately like this: Paul Senior, Paulie, Steve, and—on the same plateau—Ron and Joe Puliafico. Joe heads up our licensing and merchandising.

Ron makes sure that our build deadlines are met by overseeing the bikes that we have contracts on. Right now we build over a hundred bikes a year, a lot for a custom shop. These are high-end bikes, built from parts that we make at OCC as well as parts that come from different vendors. Those hundred-plus bikes a year include bikes built on the show.

We categorize our bikes as either theme bikes (whether they're built on or off air) or customer bikes. There have been many, many theme bikes built off the air that are just as nice as the ones built on television. For instance, we did the US Army bike, which came out phenomenally. We also did a commissioned bike for the US Air Force. These are bikes used for the promotion and recruitment of our country's armed services. Both the army and the air force proudly tour them across the country.

Private companies call us up, too. They might want to center a chunk of their marketing dollars on a custom OCC chopper build, a theme bike that represents their organization. Companies that contact us vary in size, ranging from private outfits to brand names to Fortune 500 firms. For instance, we did two Caterpillar Bikes, one for the West Coast, one for the East Coast. They're used as valuable promotional tools. Same thing with the Lincoln Bikes. We built four identical Lincoln bikes for the car company. Who knows? One day you might pass the CEO of Lincoln barreling down the highway on a Lincoln OCC theme chopper.

In addition to the theme bikes, there are customer bikes, custom bikes built for John Q. Public. It starts with a customer, whether it's an individual or a company, who is interested in having a bike built. These folks will call us up. The receptionist, who answers the phone, will hand them over to our sales manager, Mike Burkhouse. Mike will talk to potential clients to find out exactly what they're interested in. If the inquiry is a serious one, he'll go over the prices. Our bikes can range anywhere from thirty-nine thousand dollars to more than two hundred thousand (if and when Donald Trump orders that gold-plated bike), so it depends on what callers are looking for and whether or not they have any special concepts they want to build onto the bike. After customers put down a two-thirds deposit, we start brainstorming.

If customers or companies are going to spend serious money on a chopper, especially in the six-figure range, we will sit down with them and go over specifically what they're looking for. We'll throw out some ideas. If it's a theme bike as opposed to a customer bike, once we come up with a plan, Jason Pohl, our graphic designer, will draw up the bike digitally on screen and on paper. He'll set up an approval process.

If the bike is going to be built on air, we'll run the company's concept and design ideas by Paulie first to make sure he approves. Then Paulie jumps in. We'll show the final draft to the customers. Once any tweaks or changes in, for example, exhaust, colors, or logos—logos are very important!—are done, and the bike is signed off on by everyone on both sides, Ron gets geared up again. He'll order the main components—frame, motor, transmission, and so on. About a week later, once the frame shows up here, it'll go to one of our celebrated fabricators, guys like Rick Petko, Craig Chapman, or Vinnie DiMartino—whoever is assigned is by the luck of the draw. The assigned fabricator, once he receives the completed parts, will prepare for the mock-up. That is, he'll put together a dry version of the bike before it gets sent out for painting, chroming, or powder-coating.

A Jason Pohl in-house sketch idea for an OCC production bike that will come in three colors. (Photo: OCC Archives/Jason Pohl)

Before the bike is mocked up or sent out, though, Ron will sit down with everybody involved in the build. Before the frame comes in, he'll go over which bike is going to be built and who's doing it. For a customer bike, he'll reiterate the assignment and the deadline. On the higher-end bikes or corporate builds, on air or off, he'll sit down and discuss the issues as they relate to both design and fabrication, as well as deadlines and schedules. These days, we have Jason Pohl to actually draw up the bike in advance. A picture is worth a thousand words, and we've come a long way from drawings on napkins and scraps of paper. It's important to line up the designers and the builders because the act of approving a drawing and the reality of fabricating it with steel and building it are two different matters. So we'll try to anticipate any potential problems in the design that might be difficult or impossible when it ends up on the lifts under the sure hands of Rick, Vinnie, or Craig.

Sometimes Mike Burkhouse, Jason Pohl, and I might sit down and figure out which engine would look cool. Depending on the color of the bike, we'll suggest a diamond-cut engine or a polished engine. Do they want an inlay—meaning coloring in the engine—with a diamond cut? Throughout the pre-build process, we'll constantly brainstorm.

By the time the frame comes in, Ron's warriors will start on the mock-up, which includes making the wheels and doing the customization. We'll often fabricate the bike completely, making it into a rolling chassis form, with a mock-up engine in it. And from there, the fabricator pieces everything together. Once it's assembled and finished, it gets ripped apart and torn down. That's when everything goes out to our vendors. We have a powder-coater. A painter. A chromer. An inlayer. A guy who builds exhausts (if Vinnie hasn't already fabricated one of his super custom creations). We use pretty much the same core of vendors, because if you get too many parts going in and out from too many vendors in too many directions, the build gets confusing. So we try to work with the same proven folks.

The parts that we put on our bikes might come from thirty to forty different vendors. We maintain an inventory of different parts and products here in the shop. Brakes. Belt drives. Front ends. It's up to Ron to make sure our inventory is kept up. We stock plenty of parts so that when one of our builders or fabricators walks back with his cart and "goes shopping," everything's there.

As far as painters go, we try to stick with one vendor—usually Nub. When all is said and done, we've dealt with a couple of dozen entities just for parts on one bike. That's how crazy the puzzle pieces can get.

Once everything gets sent out to the painter, the powder-coater, and the chromer, how long the pieces stay out depends entirely on how much of a rush we're in. The bikes you see on TV are usually done the quickest—sometimes on a five-day turnaround, which is incredible. Our vendors jump through hoops for us. With a regular production bike, it's more like a couple of weeks, depending on how busy Ron's guys are.

Once everything comes back from the painters and chromers or powder-coaters, Ron checks his schedule to see that we're meeting our due date. Then he coordinates the final build. When everything's ready to go, he gets the assemblers ready and they start building the bike. Within three to four days, the bike is assembled. It's test-driven. Then it's ready to ride out the door.

Our guys are motivated. Nick Hansford and Christian Welter, for example, have been here for a while. They have the process down. But with custom one-of-a-kind bikes, there's always a problem here and there. A bracket might not fit. Something might have been overlooked. A measurement is off. The guys might miss something on the mock-up—which they rarely do, but it does happen. Issues come up. Something on the mock-up might have to change. For instance, you're not going to put a brake cable on a mock-up. But when you put the brake cable on the real bike, maybe you'll find that it interferes with something on the design. Those are the problems that need to be troubleshot, so we'll figure them out.

Sometimes we'll monkey with a deadline, meaning we'll need the *drop-dead* date a customer *really* needs the bike by in case we need more time. At least once a month, we'll get into a pinch with bikes. You must remember, we're not stamping out doughnuts here. Custom bikes are neither an exact science nor an assembly-line product. Ours aren't, anyway. It's the nature of the beast and the cost of success that the process and the time line fluctuate.

We get calls from a lot of businesses. If they want a bike built on the show in front of the cameras, then things get a little tricky. We can only do so many shows and so many on-air builds per season. So there's a selection process based on the nature of the company and how exciting the build will look on television. The only thing we'll out-and-out reject is nudity, alcohol-, and tobacco-related products on a bike, on air or off. We just won't do it. One guy, for instance, wanted the devil on his bike, and we wouldn't do it. We did the bike for him, but we didn't use that motif. He was fine with it.

We make the call which bikes go on *American Chopper,* but that doesn't stop companies from asking, sometimes begging, in an attempt to score millions of bucks' worth of television time and exposure as millions of eyes watch their bike being built on camera.

Sometimes a company will want to do an on-air build that we're iffy about. We once had a computer company come to us. These people wanted to do an on-air build, and it was worth a lot of dough, but we didn't bite. It didn't fit in with the feel of the show. The way they wanted us to build their bike just didn't work for us. Or if Paulie's not real keen on a build, and he doesn't think it'll fly, it doesn't matter what the money is, the idea is nixed. While we'll turn down several on-air requests, we will do most off-air builds, because building bikes is our core business.

Not all of our builds are for companies. Sometimes we'll go weeks or even a few months without doing a corporate or on-air build. Or sometimes we'll do a Senior Old School bike, something we feel like building. And not all of our on-air bike builds are corporation bikes. For instance, the Fantasy Dream Bikes that we built for four lucky riders who submitted their requests for an OCC dream chopper were ordered and paid for by Discovery. We charged them the going rate.

A huge majority of our customers are happy customers. But sometimes there are problems. For instance, color can be a bitch. We try to get the right color selection out of customers before we begin. Color is something that makes us nervous, because it's so important. Color and company logos. There have been times, one or two instances, when we delivered the bike and it wasn't the color they wanted. Sometimes customers or companies want the same color as another famous bike we've built, only to find out that the color they ordered wasn't the color they thought it was. (You may want to adjust the color on your TV, okay?) Sometimes we end up building another bike and selling the "botched" one. It's no big deal.

Corporations are the most demanding. The people at Caterpillar were meticulous about their yellow because it's as important as their logo. Yellow is their trademark. If we didn't match the yellow perfectly, it would have to be redone. Caterpillar actually had different yellows, one an Old School yellow, another a New School version. We had them pick out which yellow they wanted. But after Nubby painted it, it didn't match, so he had to repaint the whole bike. Caterpillar was paying a lot, they wanted it perfect, and we wanted it perfect. While it was close to the right yellow, close only counts in horseshoes, hand grenades, and . . . well, it wasn't on the money. So we repainted.

Nub has been with us from the very beginning. He was the guy who painted the very first Jet Bike. Nubby's very professional. He does striping, airbrushing, flames—you name it, Nubby does it. He gets everything done on time, if not ahead of schedule. Nub Grafix can handle the heavy volume, plus he's right up the road in Walden. Our chromers, ChromeMasters, are out of Nashville. They are excellent.

Only a few years ago, our wheels were done out of house. Most machining was done out of house. In the beginning, we didn't even have a lathe. Now we have a lathe as well as a host of modern machines and tools. Most of our machining today is done in-house, minus the belt drives. Anything like wheels, air cleaner covers, we do in-house. If there's a problem where something needs to be milled down, or something has to be rectified, Jim Quinn, our brilliant engineer, can figure anything out. In the beginning, I'd go home with a headache or a knot in my stomach worrying. Now I know that between our guys on the mills, the lathes, and the water jet, we'll get it done. We've come a long way with our equipment and CNC machines. (We talk about the technological advances at OCC in a later chapter.)

As far as gas tanks go, outside of a hand-tooled one-of-a-kind special tank pounded out by one of our fabricators, we find that it's just cheaper and better to have a tank company make the gas tank. (Remember, the more time and money it costs *us,* the more it costs *you,* our customer.) While we could make our own gas tanks all day long, it isn't a cost-effective use of labor and resources.

When you look at any bike, you'll see a motor, wheels, transmission, front end, frame, and pins. But there are so many more odds and ends and so many different types of parts that get used, it's mind-boggling. As a result, the motorcycle industry has grown considerably, with the parts and the custom bike builders and all the shops out there. Over the past couple of years (thanks partly to the success of *American Chopper*), the motorcycle business has taken off. Not every bike builder fabricates every single part (including companies like Harley-Davidson), so we depend on a host of smaller companies to furnish us with the quality parts we need to build custom bikes.

Computer technology has impacted OCC quite a bit. We've gone from using one laptop computer in the old shop to having an entire network set up for the staff, ranging from the fabricators making wheels to the support staff crunching numbers, doing PR, designing bikes, or building Web sites. We actually have an in-house IT person and a graphic designer. We have digitizers, which enable us to make identical parts. Even though Paulie, Mikey, and I know squat about computers, we've grown by leaps and bounds thanks to the technology that OCC utilizes.

Having *American Chopper* filming inside the shop only magnifies our operations. The show has made our tremendous growth possible, but it also adds weight. Bumping projects in favor of on-air builds. Coordinating airport pickups and bike events. Itineraries have to be set up for on-air and off-air events and appearances. Our staff need to know what Paulie, Mikey, and I are doing at all times. Between the television appearances, bike shows, and client meetings, there's much more to OCC than just building bikes now. It's very demanding for everyone. With such busy travel schedules, it's rare that Paulie, Mikey, or I are here a whole week at a time. When we're not filming, the rest of the crew gets a breather to get things done without interruption. Once the filming starts up again, it can cause delays and setbacks. But it's something we gladly live with because it was the show that helped create our bread and butter. Producer Steve Nigg and his film crew do an excellent job of letting us do our jobs, while he continually feeds raw footage to the editors and producers at Pilgrim Films in Los Angeles.

A conceptualized sketch of a yellow-flamed OCC production chopper. (Photo: OCC Archives/Jason Pohl)

Knowing that the show might not go on forever, we have lots of ideas and projects in development. Planning a line of production bikes. Putting together new clothing lines. Launching new ideas for the future. While there may not always be a TV show, we can produce our bikes, and with endless television syndication, we'll have enough high-profile exposure to keep us in the public eye. Who knows what tomorrow may bring? A different brand of media that we can't imagine today might give us a whole new level of exposure and access to potential customers. Who imagined the Internet twenty-five years ago? We know today that if the show ended tomorrow, we'd have ideas to develop and a company to continue to grow. We'll have growing pains, because if you don't have growing pains, you'd better start finding some. With the drive that everybody has here, I have no doubt we'll keep rolling well into the twenty-first century.

Most of the parts for the US Army Bike were computer-designed, then fabricated and created in-house at Orange County Choppers. (Photo: OCC Archives/Jason Pohl)

CHOPPERS IN CYBERSPACE

SENIOR:

I'm an Old School guy who knows diddly about computers. But I'm smart enough to know that I need to surround us with people who *do* know.

I need to know that we can take something designed and drawn on a computer and make it real. Computers are all well and fine. At first we used them for e-mails and booking hotel reservations. Then we took the leap. The hiring of Jason Pohl and Jim Quinn opened the door to making Orange County Choppers a new-millennium shop.

Jason, or "Pohly" as I like to call him, came on board first. Drawing motorcycles since he was six years old, he arrived with a background in computer animation and modeling for Xbox and PlayStation 2 video games. We met him while he was working on a stand-up arcade-style OCC video game. We liked his animated bike designs, which, for copyright reasons, had to be completely original. Now, what Paulie once sketched on a napkin for a bike built on the air, Jason draws on a computer screen using Adobe Illustrator. Jason can make a nice digital picture, and then create a 3-D computer model of an OCC chopper in cyberspace. But the question remains: How easy is it to take a cool computer-generated design and make it road-real? That's exactly where Jim Quinn comes in. With close to twenty years' experience as a machinist and engineer, Jim together with Jason pushed OCC—kicking and screaming—into the modern world of technology. Can we take one guy's artistic background with video games and combine it with another guy's engineering background and machine a motorcycle part out of billet aluminum that actually functions? So far the answer is yes.

Technically, a bike is nothing but a bunch of parts put together. In the old days, we got our parts at the bike shops, ponying up retail. Then once we got up to speed and started rolling out more bikes, we were able to buy our parts wholesale, which increased our profit margin. Of course we also fabricated our own custom parts like fenders and handlebars, as well as a few smaller, more detailed parts. But now we've reached the point where, after a few hours have been invested designing a part inside a computer using software programs like Mastercam and SolidWorks, we can design and stamp out our own parts using machines like CNC lathes, CNC mills, and water jets. What exactly do these computerized machines do?

Mastercam software, for instance, will place a path on the surface of metal and tell a tool precisely where to cut. *CNC* stands for "computer numeric control," and what it means to me, without getting into a lot of boring detail, is that we can produce identical parts with the push of a button as opposed to having to go to the drawing board or the parts store each time we need a part. In the case of wheels, we no longer have to send out a blank wheel to a machine shop to get a finished custom product.

With the use of CNC technology, we're able to design and build our own aluminum coil covers, sprockets, rotors, brake systems, air cleaners, point covers, ignition covers, foot pegs, shift levers, gas caps, mirrors, headlight brackets, primary covers, handlebar components like risers and dog bones, handgrips, and, best of all, wheels! Our equipment is big enough to cut wheels, but detailed enough to machine smaller things like foot pegs and every size part in between.

Technology is where the dream world meets reality, making Jason's monkey cage office and Jim's machine-filled domain the technological center of OCC. Instead of pens, pencils, and paintbrushes, Jason uses a computer. Instead of blades, grinders, and torches, Jim uses a computer. Every part that's designed for an OCC bike goes through Jim. He can turn a part design from a cartoon 3-D drawing to a real-life metal part. Jason and Jim work together on just about everything we do, from the beginning of a bike design to the creation of the parts that are handed over to the assembler who builds the bike.

Working with computers isn't error-free. There's a lot of development time and trial and error involved. Sometimes a part will be drawn and modeled only to find that practically, while it looks cool in computer 3-D, it isn't big enough or designed correctly to meet the bike's needs. So we'll go back to the computer and tweak the part bigger while keeping it as close to the original design drawing as possible. With CNC mills and lathes, we're able to make square, round, and flat parts. Just about the only parts that OCC isn't capable of making right now are the tires and the motor itself. Motors are a whole different science. While the people who furnish our motors use equipment that's very similar to ours, if not identical, the fixturing time spent on the computer wouldn't make financial sense unless we were making thousands of motors a year. Right now, making our own motors doesn't make sense. But who knows what tomorrow may bring?

Wheels, though—that's a different story. Back in the day, we'd sketch out a wheel, send it out to a machine shop with a blank wheel, and the folks at that machine shop would have someone like a Jim Quinn model our design inside their computer and use *their* machines to cut out *our* wheels. No more. Now we can craft the most intricate wheel designs in-house.

Example. We once did a cool 3-D–looking wheel on a sports car bike that we made for the son of a Middle Eastern prince. He wanted a bike that matched his car, down to full billet wheels. In other words, wheels cut not from a blank wheel but from a hunk of aluminum. Since he had the money, and we had the time, we made his custom wheels to match the jet engine turbine design of the car's wheels. A wheel can be cut in as little time as two hours. But that bike took thirty or forty hours per wheel, carved out of pure aluminum billet. A lot of time went into making fixtures to hold the individual parts and components that made up each wheel. Once we made the first wheel, the second came out a lot quicker. Since it was a one-off project, we won't make those wheels again, but it served as the best example of the use of our in-house technology taken to extremes. Thank goodness we didn't have to build that bike on air.

How do we know that what gets designed on a computer will hold up on the highway? If a wheel looks cool, how do we know that the pressure points won't collapse, making it nice to look at but completely ridiculous and dangerous to ride on?

The answer is a software program called Cosmos with a feature called "finite element analysis." This lets us design a wheel, and then model it on the computer so that we can actually apply simulated loads and strains and get a graphic readout in a color gradient of reds and greens that will tell us if the wheel has any potential trouble spots. If we run into a problem, then all it takes is throwing in a bit of radius to make the wheel more stable.

Our wheels are made of 6001 forged aircraft-grade aluminum. They have good machinability, great strength, and vigorous wear and corrosion resistance. We'll buy blank wheels with enough of a flange that we can detail whatever design we want.

For instance, on a bike we built for Criss Angel, the television illusionist and magician, Criss wanted his logo, a special A, floating inside the circle of the wheel with full three-inch flanges all the way to the outside. By using a combination of engineering and a computer program, we were able to make a wheel that was cool and structurally stable. As a result, Criss was a happy customer.

As you've probably guessed, OCC is moving toward designing and selling our own parts. We've already started selling our own line of custom wheels to bike shops and individuals with a choice of chromed, powder-coated, and polished finishes. That's because once the programming and modeling is done for any wheel design we've used—or any part, for that matter—we can easily and precisely manufacture more of the same. I see the day when a line of OCC-branded motorcycle parts can be shipped to stores around the world. That's where we're headed.

The water jet is another machine that revolutionized OCC. The water jet was our first CNC-driven machine. Other bike builders and machinists use most of these machines. You might have watched Vinnie master the water jet on *American Chopper*. Vinnie is now a certified water jet maniac. As a result, the water jet is an OCC workhorse. It's a machine where Vinnie can cut straight, round, or at angles. The water jet cuts with high-pressure water and a sand abrasive. There's no blade involved. It's like a fine stream of sandpaper running at high speed, cutting through material. The brand of water jet we use is Flow International, aka the Flow Jet. With our raw material, we can water-jet something close, fixture it onto the mill, and then cut it precisely. The water jet helps us create a lot of widgets in-house that bolt right onto the bike, like tabs and mounts, fender struts, the tabs that hold our blinkers, the risers for handlebars, flat adapter plates . . . the list is endless.

I could go on and on describing technology that has made our lives easier and our bikes more modern and precise. Our dream is to one day make every part on the bike. That day isn't so far away. Two factors figure into why we adapt certain technologies to our bike builds. One is speed. The other is cost. Anytime we can make something in-house faster than something that's shipped out to somebody, we save time. And when we save time, we save money. There's your cost factor.

Not always at odds, Senior and Paulie crack up on camera. (Photo: Martin GM Kelly)

CHAPTER 24

YOU CAN'T KEEP IT UNLESS YOU GIVE IT AWAY

PAULIE:

We once met up with a client in Kentucky at Bristol Motor Speedway during a NASCAR race. After the meeting was over, the race was set to begin. Walking through Pit Row was a thrilling experience. Jeff Gordon strolled by, and we said hello to a lot of the drivers. Since there were only a few minutes left before they dropped the flag, we needed to leave Pit Row and head up to the skybox. The speedway didn't have a tunnel under the track to the seats, so we had to hurry and cross the actual racing surface.

As my father, Mikey, and I crossed the track, it was obvious, even from a distance, that we were the Teutuls from *American Chopper.* In a chain reaction, the capacity crowd in our corner of the speedway broke into a loud cheer, then launched into a chorus of chants and hollers. As we crossed the roadway, my dad threw his fists up in the air Rocky Balboa–style. It was as if the race had started. The crowd responded with noisy cheers. Steve Moreau, who had just joined our organization, couldn't believe what he saw and heard. It made the hair stand up on the back of my neck. We weren't expecting such a reception. As we entered the stands and headed up to our seats, the screaming continued. We traded high fives with our people. We were slapped on the back. The whole section erupted. It gave me chills. Just like that day inside the Louisiana Superdome, it was a pivotal moment for our company that convinced us we *can* make a difference, and we can use our power of recognition to go on and do greater things.

We've made a tremendous impact across the board. My idea to build theme bikes caught on. As far as I know, nobody had, as part of their business model, built theme bikes on commission. There are plenty of talented bike and hot rod builders out there, but it's been our personas that have brought us to the table. It's not just the bikes themselves that have brought marketability to our company; it was the whole OCC family package that made it work.

Clients don't just buy motorcycles; they buy us. The reason our bikes and products sell is because we stand solidly behind them. It's like that NASCAR incident in Kentucky showed us: We're highly recognizable. Average Joes respond to our ethics and values and what we stand for, hard work and the American Dream. We are who we are, and that's the most important part of our package—honesty and transparency. What you see is what you get. The bike serves as the "ooh and aah" that draws you in. If it were just bikes, lots of people could do what we do. But our value-add is the Teutul name. It's about having your bike built by us on the show, then having us come out and unveil it to the people who make up the company.

First off, we don't build bikes for companies unless we believe in what they do. Our public perceives that, and corporations realize it, too. No matter which company calls us, it must meet our approval. If a company makes sense, we'll build the bike. For instance, we're not going to build a chopper for Jack Daniel's or Camel cigarettes. We're not going to build a bike for Budweiser. Not that we knock any of these companies or hold them in any judgment. They're doing what they do, and they're probably fine organizations. But cigarettes and alcohol aren't who we are, nor are they what we choose to represent with our bikes.

While conglomerates constantly scrutinize the small businesses they do business with, we turn the tables. We scrutinize *them.* Actually, *more so.* As a result, we turn down work. We could have built a bike for a girlie mag publisher. But we didn't. A major political party came forward and asked us to build them a chopper to promote their political campaign for the president of the United States! That's the impact we've achieved by taking risks and working hard. (We turned them down, but he got elected anyway.)

When we work for corporations, we not only build a theme bike, but help build morale for the company as well. Employees love it when we show up to unveil a bike. When we visit a plant, everybody's in an uproar. We're blue-collar guys who have found success. We didn't go to celebrity school. So if we seem unaccustomed to fame, we are.

While we don't wear suits, neither are we rock stars, and we're not outlaw bikers. We're not sheltered by a rock star/celebrity bubble. We show up for work every Monday morning (and Saturdays too), unprotected from the cold hard realities of everyday working life.

What justifies a business spending money on an OCC chopper? Once we build a company's bike, it goes on the road to trade shows, dealerships, and subsidiaries. In talking to the people, we've found that companies and their employees feel we've created a bike that reflects who they are and what they do to earn a living for their families. The bikes become a symbol, and a theme bike symbolizes not only a company, but also the people who make up that company, from the assembly line to the boardroom.

When we built a bike for Caterpillar, we sent the message that *we're* behind the people who build Caterpillar tractors and products. Our fans can be assured that Caterpillar is a good product. Our bikes are our bond and our endorsement. Same thing applies to Miller Electric. We built their bike because we use their welders. Same thing with Snap-on Tools and Airgas. And the US Army and Air Force. And FDNY. And the Statue of Liberty. We believe in what those companies, organizations, and symbols stand for. Our bikes tell a story, and that's what fascinates the riders, nonriders, and families who watch the show. Other builders might call our bikes hokey and corny. A lot of so-called hard-core bikers view us as cake decorators. But we know who our audience is, and if they're pleased, we're pleased. We learned long ago that you can't please everybody.

Our future looks bright. In the not-too-distant future, we'll be breaking ground on a one-hundred-thousand-square-foot headquarters up the road in Orange County that will house our current operations. It'll be our version of Teutuland, where friends and fans can visit, watch us work, and catch a bite to eat. Make a day of it with the kids and family.

Another important part of our growth and diversification plan is the selling of aftermarket parts like foot pegs, handlebars, sissy bars, custom wheels, turn signals, headlight assemblies, license plate mounts, and other parts that have appeared on some of our more famous custom cycles.

One day soon we hope to introduce a whole line of production motorcycles so that more and more riders can experience riding and owning an Orange County Chopper.

One of my father's favorite *American Chopper* moments came when we built the Christmas Bike and invited the kids and families affected by the 9/11 attack to celebrate the holidays with us at the OCC shop. We were able to hand out gifts to the kids. We enjoy working personally with charitable trusts involved with our armed forces here and overseas. That's work that feels good, and the work we want to continue to do.

At the same time that we merchandise ourselves, we're very active on the charity front. We regularly work with groups and foundations (like the Make-A-Wish Foundation) and with famous athletes, celebrities, and individuals who have set up their own aid organizations. That's because we subscribe to the old adage: "You can't keep it unless you give it away." In essence, the best part of fame is *being in a position to give.*

CHAPTER 25

Blimey! The Teutuls hold up Stonehenge for the Brits in Salisbury. (Photo: Martin GM Kelly)

MAINTAINING BALANCE

MIKE:

Sometimes it's hard to distinguish between what's real and what's a dream. The largest personal appearance we ever made was one of those moments. It happened in jolly old England with a scheduled bike run that started in London and ended up in the seaside resort of Brighton.

The plan was for us to ride rented Harleys starting at the Ace Café in London, then on into Brighton for an event that was accustomed to accommodating forty thousand visitors. Well, the event we attended drew about 120,000 people. We were supposed to be the grand marshals for the main run from London to Brighton. We led the motorcycle procession with a swarm of police bikes around us. I guess the run to Brighton went okay, but riding into town for the final stretch involved a mile-long strip that we had to get through to make it to the stage. The area in Brighton ahead of us was flooded with people waiting for us. Behind us were thousands of bike riders. We were boxed in.

Once we got in to the event, the crowd was so overwhelming, the organizers warned us that we might need to leave—not in a mean way, but because the organizers were so ill prepared for the huge reception, they were concerned. We saw that they had built this tiny stage that faced out into the English Channel and not toward the crowds that were blocking up the roadway and crowding the streets. There was room for only a few hundred people out on the beach in front of the little stage to see us. It was a joke. SNAFU. Botched.

The situation was out of control. We were stuck, pinned in, and we couldn't swim across the English Channel to get away. It was time to leave. Or more accurately, time to run.

A week before, we'd sat in a meeting in Washington, DC, with the Discovery Networks people and the British organizers of the event. We'd warned them about the crowds we were gathering in the States, yet they insisted that the British fans weren't at all like American fans.

"You have no idea what you're talking about," Paulie said. "Fans are fans."

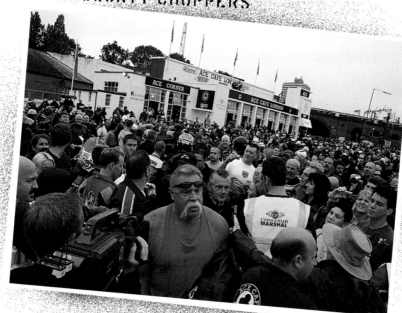

The Teutuls are mobbed at the Ace Café in
London. (Photo: Martin GM Kelly)

No, they insisted. The American tourists were the only people we needed to worry about. The rest of the crowd, the Europeans, would behave. Well, 120,000 folks showed up and they weren't all American tourists. The natives went bananas. After we got mobbed outside the Ace Café as we got on our bikes to ride to Brighton, the same lady who told us at the meeting that everything would be okay ended up getting caught right in the middle of a horde of people rushing toward us. I'll never forget the expression on her face as she got shoved around in the sea of bodies. People were reaching over her to get to us. She was freaked out. And if things at the Ace Café weren't crazy enough, it got stranger when we hit that Brighton bottleneck of humanity. Our Harleys overheated, so my father, Paulie, Steve Moreau, and I cut our engines and put the bikes down on their kickstands. We walked the rest of the way to our trailer.

After a brief stay waving and tossing a few OCC Frisbees into the crowd, we were forced to take the advice of the organizers and hightail it outta there. For the safety of our fans, and for ourselves, we had to leave.

I thought back to that day at the Louisiana Superdome, with the Fire Bike, the Black Widow, the firefighters, and the war veterans. What a long circle and cycle it's been. Now it's something to tell my grandkids.

Paulie in front of the Ace Café before leading a large pack of riders into 120,000 Brighton revelers. (Photo: Martin GM Kelly)

PAULIE:

For us to hit it big when we did, some say, "Wow, you guys got lucky." But I believe it was in His plan. Things didn't just happen. It came from hard work. So when we hit, everything kicked into gear not a day too soon, not a day too late. It was a weird domino effect that started the day we began filming the first pilot; from that point on, it fell together perfectly. Jesse James set it up to a T in 2001 by popularizing the chopper on *Motorcycle Mania.* Then we knocked it out of the park in 2002 with *American Chopper.* It was perfect timing. The chopper made an amazing comeback. After ten years of Pro Street bikes, the industry was ready for something fresh and new. But it wasn't something "new." People fell back in love with the chopper, a leftover symbol of freedom and the open road from the 1960s and the '70s. That concept had faded in the 1980s and '90s, but came roaring back in the twenty-first century when individual riders started expressing themselves with raked and stretched-out frames. I was born after the original birth of the chopper, but I'm glad to have contributed to its strong and popular resurgence.

If our company has a vision, it started with the OCC logo I drew. I designed the logo and the look of our bikes. The idea of theme building stemmed from that. When it comes down to that particular creative thread of OCC, I like to think that it came from me. My father had the push and tenacity and determination to get the business moving forward.

I believe vision is when you can see into the future. But vision is also about responding to the present tense. I credit our success to divine inspiration. The only reason I say that is because when I came up with that logo—which typified the sleek, stretched-out design of our bikes—I don't believe it came from within me. It wasn't something I could have come up with on my own. Somebody was watching over us.

I'm not a hard-core biker. My father is more so—and he's not even that hard-core. But motorcycles are much more a part of his lifestyle than they are mine. For me, the main part of my lifestyle devoted to motorcycles is my work as a designer, not as an avid rider.

Bikes are my job, my livelihood, the way I express myself creatively. Not to downplay their importance, but I'm not the guy who goes out riding to Glacier National Park for a two-week vacation. That's my father, not me. I think in the past, those differences are what he and I have mixed it up about. We've banged heads because I'm not him and he's not me.

Now I see past a lot of stuff. I see past business. As important as work is, it's not everything to me. My father and I differ in those areas. Our priorities are different. There *are* more important things to life than just money and business: Family and friends. Taking time for you. I think for my father, it's always been about business and money. When the money comes in, I say, "Now what?" Sure, you keep succeeding, which is great, and that's what we should do. But you need to maintain some balance in your life.

Everybody, including us Teutuls, struggles with finding that balance. I exhibit extreme behavior just like my father does. I'm a compulsive person just like him, and although I think I've gotten better through the years, I have that predisposition to go overboard. The alcoholism and the obsessive nature that run in my family are character traits that we were brought up to look out for. Part of it is hereditary and part of it has been drilled into my head since birth. I have that predisposition toward excess. This is why I have to keep maintaining balance in my life.

Between my father and me, I try to be the voice of reason. I'm the guy who says, "Calm down, let's talk about this." With my father, everything is in extreme freak-out maniacal mode. He's all over the place, ready to rip, ready to yell. I'm the guy who says, "Hey, let's not fight." It's what I get from my mother. And it's made me a better decision maker. I think more before I act. My father doesn't practice that restraint, although I'm hoping one day he will.

Senior takes serious pause at the cemetery at Colville (Omaha Beach) in Normandy, France. (Photo: Martin GM Kelly)

SENIOR:

I don't think I'll ever fully retire. Work is life, and I've built businesses all my life. I take enormous pride in them. In the steel business, we set out to build and we achieved our goals. And I was happy with that. At Orange County Choppers, we made progress and we made a little history.

But OCC has changed a few things in the world. How the modern-day chopper is perceived. How reality TV shows are made. Creating a new and unique business model. But those are the small things. Mostly, OCC has added fuel to the hopes and dreams of men and women. An example of how anywhere in the world, if you work hard enough and play by the rules, you can achieve your dreams and succeed. Even in the competitive corporate world, a world where the odds of success are stacked against Everyman, you can live your dreams just like my family and me.

We took an industry that was relevant to less than 1 percent of the population—motorcycles—and propelled it into the living rooms of 160 countries. The best part is this: None of it was done by design. We didn't originally intend to achieve anything more than building beautiful bikes and selling a few shirts and hats. Being able to build bikes for a living would have been reward enough. What a lucky break, being able to capitalize on fortune, hard work, and determination.

Paulie believes that our success was destined to happen. Like there was a spiritual guidance. Someone, something watching us from above. True. But Paulie also had a family and a determined father behind him. And without degrading or downplaying the faith behind his beliefs, left to our own devices, we might easily have self-destructed.

I'm a born-again Christian, too. But I believe that sometimes people confuse God's will with the potential experiences that God has in store for us. I think that God uses you as a tool. But if you don't expose yourself to the right elements and opportunities, then what good are you doing hiding inside a church, hanging out with the saved, not taking the necessary chances or risks, opting to believe instead that God will guide you on a predetermined path?

You can't be a power of example with just words and wishes. You can be a power of example only in who you are and in what you experience and learn in life. Life lessons. The way to achieve greatness is by having good and bad experiences. You have to walk it, talk it, and then live it. Look at Jesus Christ. He hung out with the riffraff, the prostitutes and the sinners. It started in the dirt. The salt of the earth. The bottom. Had you met me thirty years ago, you might not have found me worth knowing because I hadn't yet experienced the many good and bad things in my life that made me who I am.

One of the most important things I've learned in life is humility. The only way you can truly learn humility is to get your ass kicked. When you get your ass kicked enough times, after you've said *uncle* a few times, you learn respect and humility. If you've never been kicked around or hit bottom, chances are you don't know humility.

Watching the show, people think they know me. And for the most part, most of you do know me. Yet the misconceptions come from people who ask, Why do you pick on your kid? Why are you such a grouch? When the show started out, the producers made me out as the heavy. Granted, that wasn't a difficult thing to do. But they would cut out anything conciliatory that I did, making Paulie into the good guy while I played the heavy. Yet people got it. They saw through the editing, and now it's turned around. I'm no longer the heavy. I'm satisfied that people perceive me for who and what I am, other than being a moody guy. If I freak out, there's a reason, and I think the audience caught that. While the degree to which I freak out may not always be appropriate, there's a reason *why* I freak out. As a father, you come to a point in your life where it's hard to tolerate stupidity. At this stage in life's game, I've paid my dues, and what's important to me may not be important to someone younger and with less life experience. But someone needs to captain the ship. And that's me.

As a husband, the big issue between my ex-wife and me was that she (and I) spent years trying to change me. Trying to change my personality. My work habits. My relationships with my kids. We each had our own baggage, but unfortunately for her, everything she despised about me, everything she wanted me to change in my life, was the essence of what made me successful. Everything she was against was everything that helped me break through.

There are few men walking the planet today who have been as counseled as me. I went to counseling three times a week in between 12-step meetings. Believe me, a lot of it stuck. I don't regret much of it. But there came a point when I had to accept who I was. No more tweaks and adjustments.

When I reached that point, I was expected to change more and more. Deal with childhood issues and the like. I'm no angel by any means, and while I *was* receptive to change, it was time to put childish (and childhood) things aside. I hit the point of rebellion. From that day forward, I couldn't change anymore. The kids were old enough to understand and accept it, and that's when I left my home, taking the first difficult step toward the most success I've had in my life.

As far as fame goes—well, I never look at my situation in life in terms of being famous. I look at it as an accomplishment that I have managed my life and business despite the fame and attention. Fame is a dangerous tool that God puts in your hands. Had I experienced fame at Paulie's age, I would have been dead within a year. I would have had every hooker. I would have bought the best coke. The best heroin. Life would have been one big party. I would have blown it big-time. I'd be gone. No doubt.

I have my hopes and dreams centered on being a businessman and a father. When you're a father and a businessman, you want to give your kids the opportunity to run the family business, but at the same time, you don't want to give them the opportunity to destroy it. So you structure your affairs in a way so your loved ones are protected from themselves. As a father, ultimately you want to provide what's best for your family. But it's also the classic syndrome of being an enabler, the scenario where loving someone to death doesn't necessarily work, either. Ideally, I'd want my kids to be tuned in to what's going on. Help put them in a position where down the road they're familiar with everything that goes on. But you can't force-feed involvement and commitment.

Businesses can't run themselves. Not now. To be on top of your business, you have to know what's going on. Either you or someone you trust with your life and your family's future. When it comes to business and family, you can't pick and choose a time for commitment, or when you want or don't want to be involved. If I want to go fishing and something erupts—I can't go fishing. Those less committed will.

Although I've had businesses for thirty years, I choose to continue learning. I've learned that sometimes I have to sit on the sidelines and listen. It's not about power. It's the need to delegate and focus.

There was a time when I was the secretary, the painter, the fabricator, and the installer. Then at night, I got on the phone and hustled business. As you get older, and if you're lucky enough to have good people in various positions of responsibility, you start to learn from them. That's a luxury I now have, being surrounded by bright people, New and Old School.

When the door didn't work, I tried the wall. My life has been about perseverance. But trusting a general manager or a licensing person or a marketer—that was a transition that was very, very difficult for me. When I had to start putting my trust in other people, it was a hard thing to do. *I* was the guy in charge of everything. It was hard to let go and let people just do it and trust that they could do it right. That concept took me forever to digest. I felt that I had to (a) do it myself, or (b) make damn sure someone else did it right. I was hands-on, too hands-on. Over the past years, though, I'm seeing the advantages of letting go. Proof you can teach an Old Schooler new tricks.

My wish is for the legacy of Orange County Choppers to live on. But I've done more than wish. We've created an infrastructure. I once thought that if I died tomorrow, it would be a disaster. The end of a dream. Not now. Not with the team we've assembled. The business will continue, God willing, in the excellent hands of the young and the brave. Whether I'm alive or dead. Whether or not we have a weekly television show. Whether or not Paulie or Mikey chooses to take the reins. That's why we've built this company so quickly, why we've gone from six employees to sixty (and counting) in only a few years. No one person can destroy us now. One monkey can't stop the show. Now that we're rolling, though, that doesn't mean I'm not going to continue to raise hell. You know me better than that.

I shout because intimidation has gotten me a long way. This is the business world. If you can intimidate, you intimidate. Sometimes you can't get people's attention unless you're all the way in their faces. I've tried not shouting, but you know what? Shouting works. I come from the streets, not the classroom. I was never blessedly meek. I never went to that school. If I've got something to say, I'm saying it.

It comes down to this. You can take the boy out of the country, but you can't take the country out of the boy. Ten years ago, I was climbing ladders with railings on my back. Welding, loading, and installing. Hanging structures and running up and down ladders. I was the physical guy. Never afraid of hard work. Never sat in the office. I was out humping steel. Instead of using a crane, I would throw two oxygen tanks on my back and carry them up the ladder. Or I'd climb a rope instead of a ladder.

If you look at me as a person, the good outweighs the bad, a hundred to one. My heart is a lot bigger than my voice. If I yell, I yell for a reason. I yell from my heart. No one has a softer heart than I do. I give my people plenty of opportunities, benefits of the doubt, as well as second and third chances.

David Letterman once joked on his show that presumably I do nothing. People across America laughed. I laughed right along with them. But I know there's a handful of loved ones who know exactly what I do at Orange County Choppers. What they don't show you on TV is me, wide awake at five o'clock in the morning, lying in bed thinking about what's going on today, next week, next month, and next year. I may not be the guy pounding steel anymore, but if you equate what I do now mentally with what I did then physically, it's a lot harder now than when I was trying to do everything. Believe me. I'm working harder now than I've worked in my life. That's saying something.

APPENDIX

SENIOR:

Bikes are like kids. You never know how they're going to turn out. Here's just a sample of some of our favorite commissioned bikes, designed by Paulie and our graphic designer Jason Pohl (pronounced *Pool*); we've added blow-by-blow breakdowns. Some you've seen on television, some you haven't. Notice the detail in the descriptions. That's because there's a lot to these bikes. Designed to be appreciated in depth. In addition to the bike photos, we've included some of Jason's original design drawings—something our fans have never seen outside the walls of OCC.

ORANGE COUNTY CHOPPERS

*The **I, Robot** Bike commissioned by Twentieth Century Fox for the film starring Will Smith fit well with the look, set design, and futuristic theme of the hit movie. (Photo: OCC Archives)*

ORANGE COUNTY CHOPPERS

The Space Shuttle Tribute Bike was built for
NASA and has many references to the space
program hidden throughout its design.
(Photo: OCC Archives)

THE SPACE SHUTTLE TRIBUTE BIKE

The NASA bike was a fun bike for us to work on. Everyone at OCC was psyched about it. Notice the space shuttle gas tank. The rear fender has a tail with brake flaps. The shift linkage says DISCOVERY, which is the name of the space shuttle. The American flag is on the ignition cover. The primary cover has two circles, which are actually "NACA" ducts, invented by NASA back when it was known as NACA, the National Advisory Committee for Aeronautics. The ducts suck in air. There are similar ducts on old Camaros and on the sides of airplanes. They're used as a way to cool the bike's clutch and transmission. The front down tube was replaced by a custom CNC'ed (which stands for "computer numerical controlled") NASA logo. On the back is a quote from President George W. Bush: OUR JOURNEY INTO SPACE WILL CONTINUE. The mirrors have NASA logos. The handlebars are a one-off OCC creation. Nub Grafix did the paint job.

There's stuff hidden all over the bike, like MIKEY RULES on the side, in tiny letters. The exhaust is a tri-exhaust like NASA uses. The air intake has the same mission patch that NASA uses. The foot controls are a lot like those out of a space shuttle. The wheels are spinners. The six different space shuttles that were made are featured on the wheels. The disc brake is fashioned and painted to look like the earth and outer space, which was painted by Nub. Note: Jason Pohl wore a lab coat and safety glasses while working on this bike.

I, ROBOT BIKE

This is one of OCC's most popular bikes, often cited by customers who order bike builds. This bike was present for the premiere of the Will Smith movie of the same name. The gas tank was propped up on top of a backbone that you are able to see under. Paulie picked out the Roger Goldhammer front end with Euro component headlights. The wheels came from Xtreme Machine. The two-into-one exhaust system crosses through to the left side and comes out the primary. The motor is an H&L 131 with some crazy-ass air intake. Justin at JB Graphics worked on the paint job while Rick Petko fabricated the tank. The frame was by Racing Innovations, made to Paulie's sketches. Will Smith wanted something spacey for the premiere, and he got it, low and long. The whole thing was chromed. Vinnie made the front fender on our water jet back when we were in the old shop at the Ironworks.

ORANGE COUNTY CHOPPERS

*A second look at the **I, Robot** Bike from another angle. (Photo: OCC Archives)*

ORANGE COUNTY CHOPPERS

An OCC designer sketch of the Cherokee Nation Casino Bike, whose design had to be officially sanctioned by a special tribal council. (Photo: OCC Archives/Jason Pohl)

CHEROKEE NATION CASINO BIKE

The Cherokee Nation Casino is based out of Tulsa. We worked long and hard on this bike. Before the tribe approved it, there were six different versions presented. The tribe members were particular about their design, so it took about two years from start to finish to get this bike built. We used a standard frame, while the bodywork was designed to resemble a Cherokee hawk. The gas tank signifies a hawk diving through the sky on fire. It's very 3-D looking. Jason Pohl worked on this with Rick Petko, Craig Chapman, and Ty Kropp. The rear section was originally designed on construction paper, then digitized and cut out on the water jet. Craig, our fabricator, once again pieced it together like a puzzle. The fender looks like something out of a Batman movie. The pipes were cut on a water jet machine with a twenty-inch radius. The handlebars are drag bars. The motor is an H&L 131 with a Baker six-speed. The wheels on this bike represent the Cherokee Nation Casino's chip as well as their logo. The stars are spinners.

The bike has many layers of detail. For instance, the front fender has arrows arced around the tire. The front arrowheads were actually massaged by hand out of aluminum, using an air widget, which took an entire day. The rear struts are chrome feathers. Alligator Bob from Illinois made the seat using a basket-woven pattern. This was such a hot bike, we at OCC were sad to see it leave. I actually took this bike out and cruised on it before it left Orange County. It rips.

THE MILITARY AUCTION BIKE/MODERN

This bike was originally an idea to help raise money for the families of soldiers killed in action during the most recent Iraq war. This was one of two bikes built for a military charity auction: one by Paulie, one by me. This is Paulie's build, a modern bike. It started out as a possible prototype for our production bike, but it soon got a little too detailed for mass production. The bike features the very first OCC triple trees, which connect the fork tubes. The frame has an arc rear that Jason Pohl drew. Racing Innovations made it.

The wheels are extravagant, with a Ben-Hur, 3-D style. There were close to sixteen pieces to the front wheel alone. The wheels were nicknamed Kitten Killers because they spun out past the perimeter of the tire. I didn't like the name, so we changed it. Above the tribal-style primary cover is a Made in the USA shift linkage. Above that is an OCC dagger coil cover housing the ignition. The motor is an H&L 131 with a Baker six-speed. Paulie wanted to keep the exhaust hidden, so we ran a straight simple exhaust and dumped it out onto the tail. Paulie put his initials on the air intake.

ORANGE COUNTY CHOPPERS

The Modern Military Auction Bike designed by Paulie for a special air force family charity auction. (Photo: OCC Archives)

ORANGE COUNTY CHOPPERS

*The Old School counterpart to the Military Auction
Bike designed by Senior for the same air force
charity auction. (Photo: OCC Archives)*

THE MILITARY AUCTION BIKE/
OLD SCHOOL

This is my own Old School entry into the military bike auction—a funky, psychedelic Knucklehead. The wheels on this bike were internally nicknamed Nipple Biters, but I later changed the name to the Paul Senior Series. The bike has straight-shot pipes on it, while the seat acts like a spring when you sit on it. It's a very narrow bike with a coffined Rick Petko tank on it. The wheels have a high-gloss red powder-coat finish. The primary covers are as intense as the wheels. The front end is based on a classic car front-end look called a Leaf Spring. I went with gold, red, silver, and brown. It's definitely different.

SOLIDWORKS BIKE

SolidWorks is a company that we approached for our 3-D modeling needs when we began our OCC exclusive parts line. Everything from air intakes to wheels to shift linkages—any small part that comes out of our CNC machines—generally goes through our SolidWorks program at some point. The CNC machine is a mill that moves very fast at ten thousand rpms. SolidWorks is a modeling computer software company. The bike they wanted us to build for them was for SolidWorks World, their convention. The bike took us a couple of months to design. There's an exposed backbone on the gas tank, which was chromed. There's a Roger Goldhammer front end, the same type of front end we used on the *I, Robot* and Criss Angel Bikes. We created a custom one-off headlight bracket that hooks onto an Arlen Ness bracket. The rear end on this bike is like a *T. rex:* mean, sharp, and graphically intense. We wanted the bike to make a statement: "SolidWorks can be used to make motorcycles."

The SolidWorks bike marked the first time we made our own wheels. The ground-pounders on the exhaust shoot out six-inch flames, so that when you start up the bike, everyone looks. It's got a 300mm rear tire with a three-and-a-half-inch front tire. Nub Grafix did the paint job, which was designed to be minimal—as opposed to a busy paint coat—because we wanted to show off the form and function of the bike.

ORANGE COUNTY CHOPPERS

Some of the coolest OCC choppers are never seen on TV. This is a bike commissioned by SolidWorks, a software company OCC uses to design its parts. (Photo: OCC Archives/Jason Pohl)

US ARMY BIKE

The folks at the Pentagon commissioned the United States Army Bike. It became one of the most intense bikes ever built by OCC. It was specifically designed to help boost morale for the troops overseas and was to be used for recruiting. OCC worked closely with Major Michael Jason from the US Army, who spent time in Iraq commanding the troops. Major Jason wanted this bike to look like it could run through a brick wall and keep on going, a real killing machine. After we threw a few ideas at him, he told us to run with them. We wanted the bike to seem undetectable by radar, so we gave it a flat mechanical look. We came up with the design after referencing pictures of Apache helicopters and Humvees.

There are vents under the fenders and vents on the headlights. Six grenades decorate the down tube, taken from a GQRS (grenade quick-release system). The bike features custom-made foot pegs, forward controls, and floorboards. A cross-through exhaust system gives the bike a unique sound, like thunder when it's started up. The oil tank was made to look like one of the ammo boxes found on top of Humvees that are capable of shooting .50-caliber rounds at tanks. Wrapped around the bike are 223 rounds on both sides. We added an OCC air intake.

There's an M4 machine gun on the side of the bike that's removable. The M4 is the standard-issue machine gun that the US military is using right now. On the opposite side of the bike is a detachable bayonet that fixes to the end of the machine gun. The army sent us a blue-barreled practice weapon, the blue signifying "dummy," which we touched up to look real. The firing pin had already been removed, so it's no longer an operable weapon. The rear fender, gas tank, headlight, and front fender were templates made from SolidWorks that our designer Jason Pohl created, which were then water jetted out. Our fabricator, Craig Chapman, ended up with a lot of pieces that he had to put together like a puzzle.

The wheels were cut here at OCC. At first we were going to add machine guns to the wheel design, but decided later against it. So we put in bolts around the wheels to resemble a tank. To match military design, it was very important that the spokes were black and the outside perimeter of the wheel was painted green with added black bolts. Everything on this bike was flat-painted. The finish was an eggshell color that Nub Grafix did.

There are tiny rivets and American flags hidden around the bike—in fact, there are additions throughout that only a military person might pick up on. The DUTY 1 stencil is an army saying, placed on the front of the vehicle and the rear. Also on the rear fender is a claymore bag with a clip bag attached. There's a little black square on the back, an infrared signal device. (If you saw this while wearing night-vision goggles, you would know that the vehicle is friendly.) The mirrors were made at OCC. The handlebars were a newer technique we used that resembles a railing system on weaponry, making it able to mount scopes or night-vision goggles.

The whole idea of the bike was to illustrate the "New Army." Major Jason gave us the latest camouflage pattern featured on the seat, a digital camouflage made up of tiny little boxes. The ignition cover is an American flag in olive green and flat black. The front tire peeks through the front fender. We're pretty sure the US Army Bike doesn't meet street-legal codes. We're also pretty sure the army doesn't care.

ORANGE COUNTY CHOPPERS

Surely the most ominous OCC chopper ever built. Specially commissioned by the US Army, it's a war machine on wheels complete with grenades, bayonet, and standard-issue machine gun. (Photo: OCC Archives)

ORANGE COUNTY CHOPPERS

The Caterpillar Bike, commissioned by the famed tractor and heavy equipment manufacturer, was designed to look like it could drive through any construction site and keep on truckin'. (Photo: OCC Archives)

CATERPILLAR BIKE

OCC traveled to Peoria to research design ideas for this very special bike. Paulie wanted a real industrial look, so we went with a square tubing frame. The paint was flat and powder-coated, dull looking because we wanted the bike to look like it was at home rolling through a construction site. The bike has a sixteen-inch-radius front wheel, very stubby, while the wheels resemble the inner workings of a Caterpillar, with gears and stuff. The gas tank is rounded, and the exhaust is a two-into-one Rick Petko special with the popper on top, making the bike look like an awesome Old School tractor. The bike doesn't need a kickstand, because the floorboards were made of half-inch steel; just lean the bike over on either side, and it stays up.

Caterpillar was a cool company to do a bike for. Their logo was recognizable, but they were very particular about the shade of yellow. The bike is short, thick, and bulky with a mechanical presence, and was a very smooth build. Jim Quinn and Jason Pohl machined out the wheels and added bolts straight from the factory that say CAT. There's absolutely no chrome on the bike. It has an inverted front end, and the gas tank is vented to emulate heavy equipment that needs to breathe. The front grille cover, made to look like an actual Caterpillar, was cut and tapered on our water jet so that the cuts came in at an angle. It looks like an actual Caterpillar grille.

NEW YORK YANKEES BIKE

The New York Yankees Bike was created for the Jorge Posada Foundation supporting families affected by craniosynostosis, a birth defect that causes abnormally shaped skulls in infants. If this bike were to be auctioned off again, it would be the most expensive bike we've built. The air cleaner has the classic Yankees logo, while the oil tank takes on the shape of a baseball (with Paul Junior's signature on it). We created a baseball bat exhaust. On the rear axle cover is 39 AMERICAN PENNANTS. On the other side is Yankee Stadium, followed by 26-TIME WORLD SERIES CHAMPIONS. The wheels feature three crossed baseball bats with the New York Yankees logo embossed and chromed with epoxy inlay. The handlebars are baseball bats. The point cover also has a New York Yankees logo on it. The rear struts holding up the rear fender say NEW YORK. Since we didn't want straight up-and-down pinstripes (because that would have looked god-awful), the striping goes from one vanishing point toward infinity, shooting across the bike. Nub Grafix ran with that idea. Before Nub clear-coated the tank, Mikey took the tank on the road to Milwaukee and had the players, manager, and coaches sign the tank.

ORANGE COUNTY CHOPPERS

ORANGE COUNTY CHOPPERS

*The Airgas Old School Bike utilizes a gas
tank made from a vintage acetylene tank
flipped upside down. (Photo: OCC Archives)*

AIRGAS OLD SCHOOL BIKE

Airgas makes welding products that we use at OCC, from gases to cutting torch tips. They're a family-owned company. They commissioned two custom bike builds: an Old School bike to pay homage to the company's past, and a modern bike in honor of the company's future. For the Old School version, they wanted spoke tires using their old logo. The bike was done in company colors, teal and white. We decided on a cream white. The bike features an acetylene tank flipped upside down, which the company provided us with. The Old Schooler has a Springer front end; the wheels have radial spokes. There's a unique exhaust system that rips around the rear tire. Rick Petko was the chief fabricator on this bike. We used one of our OCC shift linkages. There's a sissy bar on the back. The bike uses a 10-up, 8-out bike frame, ten inches higher and eight inches farther out than a standard Harley.

AIRGAS MODERN BIKE

This is the modern counterpart Airgas commissioned. The wheels are now known as our Junior Series wheels. The frame is a 6-up, 7-out rigid frame. Craig Chapman and Rick Petko both worked on this bike as fabricators. We added a one-off OCC custom air intake cleaner. The whole bike has a fifty-three-degree rake in the front with an Eddie Trotta front end. Stainless Creations made the exhaust system with an H&L 131 motor and a right-side drivetrain Baker six-speed. On the rear fender, there are buried taillights. There's an OCC tweak bar on the front with Accutronix forward controls.

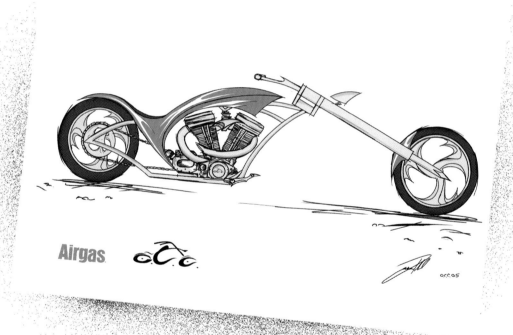

A preliminary sketch of the Airgas Modern Bike, the companion design to the Airgas Old School chopper. Airgas makes products regularly used in the shop, from gas canisters to torch tips. (Photo: OCC Archives/Jason Pohl)

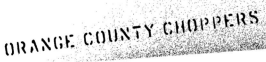

Paulie designed the Lincoln Bike in conjunction with the debut of Lincoln's first truck, the Mark LT. This is one of Paul Jr.'s personal favorites and a reason why he is heralded as one of the finest bike designers in the world. (Photo: OCC Archives)

LINCOLN BIKES

This is one of Paulie's favorite bike designs, modeled after Lincoln's Mark LT truck. It has an Eddie Trotta front end and sports an independent gas tank cut in half and flipped to the side. The gas tank was digitized and patterned and recessed again and again, then sent out and chromed. We got actual decals from Lincoln to put on the bike so we could pull off the exact logo. The front wheel has gears inside it. When it rolls, the logos tumble. There's a front grille with a Lincoln logo, plus Lincoln logos hidden throughout the bike and on the primary cover. The exhaust is a two-into-one that curves and hooks around the rear tire. The oil tank has chrome accessories. The bike's deep, dark maroon-red paint job and chrome look rich and gorgeous. The motor-mount was a one-off OCC build with a Lincoln logo. Other accessories include Accutronix forward controls and Avon wheels. With its gooseneck frame, the bike has a long, cool, classy look to it.

CRISS ANGEL BIKE

Criss Angel has his own hit TV show on A&E called *Mindfreak.* He's always ridden Harleys. Occasionally, he'll make them disappear on his show. Criss ordered a bike to ride and film for the intro of his show. He's into spiderwebs. He came to us wanting a cross between the *I, Robot* and Black Widow Bikes, the Black Widow being one of Paulie's favorites. We were up for the challenge. The bike came naturally to us: Paulie and Jason Pohl hammered out the design and concept in two hours.

The wheels feature Criss's unique logo. The air intake is another one of his logos, fashioned after a skull he wears on a diamond-encrusted necklace. The front end of the bike is by Roger Goldhammer. The frame is chromed and black with spiderweb accents. The fabricators were Mike Ammirati and Craig Chapman, who tag-teamed and knocked the bike out in less than a week, amazing time. Unlike the *I, Robot,* this gas tank drops down below the frame. This is a very long bike with webbing on top of the gas tank. The primary cover says MINDFREAK.

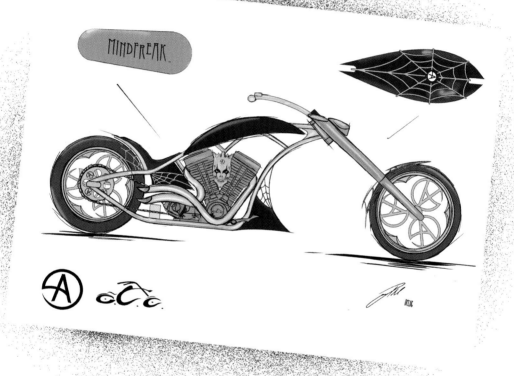

Design sketches for a bike commissioned by and built for illusionist/magician and A&E television personality Criss Angel. (Photo: OCC Archives/Jason Pohl)

>